8 Figure Owner

8 Figure Owner

How Our Clients Are Building World-Class Ecommerce Brands

Robby Switzer

©2024 All Rights Reserved. No portion of this book may be reproduced, stored in a retrieval system, or transmitted in any form or by any means-electronic, mechanical, photocopy, recording, scanning, or other-except for brief quotations in critical reviews or articles without the prior permission of the author.

Published by Game Changer Publishing

Paperback ISBN: 978-1-964811-39-0

Hardcover ISBN: 978-1-964811-40-6

Digital: ISBN: 978-1-964811-41-3

www.GameChangerPublishing.com

Read This Firsts

Just to say thank you for buying and reading my book, I would like to give you a few bonus free gifts, no strings attached!

To Download Your Free Gifts, Scan the QR Code:

8 Figure Owner

*How Our Clients Are Building
World-Class Ecommerce Brands*

Robby Switzer

www.GameChangerPublishing.com

From the Author

Dear Online Store Owner,

If you're looking to skyrocket revenue, regain family time, and build lasting wealth, this book is dedicated to you.

There is a way to grow your business that is easier, simpler, and much more effective than the methods everyone else is using. And here's the best part: **you don't need to do any of these things**:

- Shout Outs & Giveaways: They're expensive and unnecessary.
- Daily Posting: You don't need to post daily to grow your sales.
- Expensive Experts: Stop giving your profit away to agencies that overpromise and underdeliver.
- Expensive Apps: You don't need a hundred costly Shopify apps.
- Influencers & Affiliates: Also expensive and unneeded.
- Tactical Mastery: You don't need to become an expert at building, running, and scaling ads.

Imagine for a moment...

It's 1:45 p.m. You log into Shopify and see that for the 37th day in a row, you've already easily surpassed your daily sales goal. You wrap up work earlier than usual to hit the gym. Your first family vacation in over a year is only a week away! As the sun warms you through the windshield and you put on your sunglasses, you realize it has been months since:

- You felt the money you put toward ads was meaningless, not knowing if there was really even an ROI.
- When it comes to growing your sales, you didn't know what to work on, how to work on it, or if it would even matter.
- Your stomach hurts from always spending and never earning.
- Your kids were trying to tell you something, only for it to go in one ear and out the other because you were "solving" or "figuring out" what needs to happen with the store.
- As you merge lanes and your favorite song comes on, you have a quiet and peaceful moment of pure gratitude because:
- Your vision is crystal clear and in perfect alignment with the life you want for you and your family.
- Your plans to accomplish that vision are in motion, regularly tracked, on target, and mostly delegated to a team you trust.
- You sleep well knowing that month over month, your revenue, bank account, customer base, 5-star reviews, and freedom to step away from the computer are growing.

Sounds like a dream, right?

Well, it's not. It's 100% possible when you have the right tools and resources at your side. If you're ready to grow sales and reclaim your time so you can be more generous and present with your loved ones, this book is for you.

You won't regret it!

With gratitude,
Robby Switzer

Table of Contents

Chapter 1 – Building an Ecom Brand: What It Means (And What It Doesn't) 8
Chapter 2 – Crafting Your Reality vs. Chasing Your Dreams 8
Chapter 3 – Engineering Success: Calculating Realistic Moves Instead of Hoping for 10x 8
Chapter 4 – Rich Brand, Poor Brand: Achieving Real Wealth in Ecommerce 8
Chapter 5 – Unlocking the Sales Frenzy: How to Build a Brand and Create Content That Converts Like Crazy 8
Chapter 6 – The Secret to Bulletproofing Your Sales 8
Chapter 7 – Commanding Attention and Building an Endless Ocean of Traffic 8
Chapter 8 – Multiplying Returns With the Right AOV Strategy 8
Chapter 9 – LTV Alchemy: Eight-Figure Customer Retention Secrets 8
Chapter 10 – Putting It All Together 8
Introduction 1

Introduction

We've all seen the stat that 90% of ecommerce businesses fail in fairly short amounts of time. But why? And what's the difference between the ones that struggle and the eight-figure powerhouses?

Everyone has their own flavor of success, but I'm guessing, like most brand owners I've met, you're holding this book because you want some version of the following:

Revenue—and not just revenue, but profit.

Profits that climb harder than a squirrel on an espresso binge who's just seen a delightful lump of acorns. Profits that allow you to invest back into your brand and become the Lululemon of your vertical. Profits that allow you to hire a world-class team capable of keeping performance on track so you can do that wildly expensive or simply meaningful thing you've been wanting to and not worry about your ROAS getting sudden-onset bipolar syndrome and draining your bank account.

Put more plainly, we all want to grow sales, achieve market dominance, and enjoy personal freedom while an expert team of proven practitioners pushes our vision forward in perfect alignment with our brand, goals, and values.

Maybe you're well on your way to doing that. Maybe you're just a few tweaks from being there.

But maybe you've picked up this book because things aren't going so well at the moment and you do sometimes worry about being one of the nine out of ten who will fail. Or maybe you wonder if what you're doing will ever have the ability to create real wealth for you and your family. Maybe you're tired of the work it takes to keep it all from falling apart, and you want to trade that sick feeling in your stomach for real progress that isn't just a small, meaningless win but progress that is undeniably noticeable in your bank account.

If it's the latter, we've all been there. A business owner rarely has the mental space or energy to perfectly accommodate all the needs of their daily operations, let alone have the capacity to get outside of the day-to-day to chart a successful path off the current plateau and into the next growth phase (more on this in Chapter 1).

Meetings, content planning, photoshoots, returns, exchanges, marketing performance, and financial data analysis lead to best guesses and stressful inventory orders. On any given day, modern brand founders have a lot to keep up with. But that's not all; they need to somehow reserve enough bandwidth to stay on top of an industry that changes overnight and trends that evolve faster than a 14-year-old watching a hundred videos on TikTok and somehow do the research and development needed to strategically stay one step ahead of their competitors.

Before I go on, who am I, and why should you care about what I have to share with you?

My name is Robby Switzer.

Over the last eight years, my brother-in-law, Daniel Stafford, and I went from being Alaskan fishermen with no marketing know-how to co-founders of a thriving multimillion-dollar ad agency, employing 50 full-time people and helping our clients generate $600 million across 21 ecommerce niches (at the time of writing). We built families, loved our lives, and accumulated significant wealth, including a million dollars stashed away in the bank… and then all hell broke loose.

We went through 18 months of disasters, including major health issues, crippling anxiety, miscarriages, betrayals, lawsuit scares, and a massive, unstoppable revenue nosedive, leading to near-bankruptcy and a huge pile of debt, all while trying to be good leaders, family men, friends, and guys who truly want to do business in an honorable way. It didn't matter how much help we got or how hard we tried to fix our problems; we couldn't stop the bleeding.

It was miserable. We lost many clients, had to fire close friends, and leveraged our homes and personal finances to stay in the fight.

We lost almost everything—except for our conviction that even though we couldn't see it, something good would come out of this situation. This one thing gave us the hope, strength, and grace to keep showing up and face the suffering day after day.

I'm happy to say that things are going much better today. Gradually, we rebuilt our business into something remarkable. Now, our company isn't just another agency claiming to be God's gift to digital marketing or the best thing to happen to every business on the planet. Instead, because of our challenges—not in spite of them—we are uniquely positioned to help ecommerce brand founders increase their revenue.

We were knocked down, got back up, and wrote our own victory story. We stood with clients in their darkest hour and helped them survive and thrive.

Not even those fancy Silicon Valley venture capitalists have had the unique opportunity to immerse themselves in as many Shopify stores and ad accounts as we have. Day after day, year after year, we've maniacally tested and discovered what makes brands tick and drives their customers to buy, and we've built a clear understanding of how to beat the odds. We're sick of the stat that declares nine out of ten brands will fail, and we're here to turn the tide one brand at a time.

By the end of this book, my goal is not just for you to have a much better understanding of what it looks like to be an eight-figure brand, but also for you to learn several practical steps you can take immediately to shift your trajectory in that direction.

Are you ready?

CHAPTER 1

Building an Ecom Brand: What It Means (And What It Doesn't)

Welcome to the wild world of ecommerce, where consumers spend trillions of dollars every year, turning ordinary people into millionaires. This is likely why being an online seller is as common as seeing a dog in a park.

But here's the thing: the fact that billions of hungry buyers are shopping on the internet every day doesn't mean that all who set up shop online are destined for glory. There's a big difference between those who are building brands and those who are simply selling online.

Take, for example, our friend running a kitchen supply business. After years of comfortably selling from a physical store, COVID-19 threw a curveball and stripped them of their ability to sell in person, pushing them to build a website and take orders online. Suddenly, their trusty storefront, located on a busy road, and word-of-mouth marketing were as useful as a chocolate teapot. But honestly, the thought of reaching not just local buyers but even a fraction of a percent of the total buyers was pretty dang exciting for them.

Their game plan? Run ads to an online store with affordably priced, well-known products and hope for the best—sounds like a bulletproof strategy, right? Here's the problem: without a solid brand behind them, they were just another face in the crowd that nobody cared about, just one price cut away from being undercut by the big guys (like Amazon or Walmart) who have the means to play the price game better than anyone and actually strategize on how to put people like this kitchen store out of business. The worst part about merely selling online is that the reward for the few who do have success with this approach is a big, fat target on their back. When deep-pocketed sellers see a commodity selling well, they start strategizing on how to take those sales for themselves.

In one case, Amazon stomached over $200 million in losses over about two years to muscle out Diapers.com, a quickly growing startup. The baby-supply brand was figuring out how to deliver bulky, low-margin diapers profitably, with strategically placed warehouses and overnight shipping that made Amazon's delivery look slow.

Amazon, seeing their success, slashed diaper prices to be more competitive and appealing to customers. They accumulated heavy losses as they waited for their nasty plan to unfold.

Sure enough, Diapers.com's growth started to slow. They raised cash to keep up with Amazon's deep pockets, but it was like trying to fill a leaking bucket. Amazon was bleeding money like crazy, but it was all part of their plan to win the market over. Eventually, Diapers.com, running low on cash and options, waved the white flag and signed a merger agreement with Amazon.

Long story short, if you're just here to sell products, you will lose to somebody who has more patience and money. Thankfully, there's a way for you to effectively compete with the best of the best, make tons of money, and protect yourself against this kind of thing. But before we jump there, let's cover a more subtle version of "selling online," as opposed to building a brand that is actually a lot more common than the commodity example above: dropshippers.

Now, to be clear, I am all for dropshipping as a logistical mechanism for simplicity and efficiency. I also believe that brands that outsource their fulfillment to a credible third-party logistics provider (3PL) are making a wise decision and establishing a solid foundation for scaling when their marketing and sales eventually take off.

What I am not all for, and what I am referring to here when I say "dropshippers," is the group of people who think running a successful ecommerce business is as easy as finding generic but trending products on Alibaba and pressing a few buttons. I am referring to the people who view Shopify stores as side hustles and customers as faceless transactions.

What dropshippers don't understand is that products alone don't make a brand or even add much value to the world. The feelings, the story, the connection, the desires a specific product fulfills, and the pain that those products help people avoid are what build value and true riches in ecommerce.

For instance, let's consider a brand like Chubbies. In 2011, Tom Montgomery and some college buddies turned heads on a Fourth of July weekend with the vintage shorts they were wearing. But shorts are a dime a dozen, right? More specifically, in an industry chock full of rich competitors, selling short shorts that went out of style in the 1970s at a premium price sounded insane.

But Chubbies isn't just selling shorts; they're selling a weekend lifestyle, a ticket to the fun train. They've built a brand that makes their customers feel like the life of the party, even if they're just grilling in the backyard. How? They offer a real brand that's more than just a product—it's an experience, a feeling, according to Montgomery. "We're just a small company doing big things. The story we're telling is big, emotional, and it's our dream. We began seeing that our customers are just as passionate about these things as we are."

Chubbies sales grew from $2.4 million in 2012 to $44.1 million in 2020, and in September 2021, Solo Stove acquired Chubbies for $129 million. Annual revenues are now north of $100 million.

Most people in ecommerce will try to sell products and fail. Some will discover a short-lived opportunity to sell products without a real brand, only to make a few bucks from customers without loyalty and eventually be beaten by someone willing to sell the same product for cheaper.

Meanwhile, people who understand the importance of building a brand are launching new companies every day, creating new markets, transforming ones that have been around forever, building true wealth for themselves, and adding boatloads of value to their customers. Brands like Kylie Cosmetics, Gymshark, Fashion Nova, Allbirds, Athletic Greens, ColourPop, and Ruggable will continue to grow their revenue by creating raving fans who are hungry to pay more for their products rather than buy comparable alternatives elsewhere.

If you're here with the mindset that simply listing products online and running a few ads is enough or that ecommerce success is about undercutting the competition on price, I'm afraid I'm not the guide you need. The ecommerce landscape is littered with the remnants of these short-lived endeavors.

However, if you're the visionary who sees beyond the horizon, who understands that ecommerce is not just about transactions but about creating connections, telling stories, building communities around a brand, and mobilizing the right marketing strategy to profitably amplify it to millions of people, then you've come to exactly the right spot.

Let's be clear: although I am going to show you strategies and tactics that will make the previously impossible seem easy-peasy, this path isn't about the easy sell. It's about the long game, where value, authenticity, and customer relationships are paramount. It's about understanding that in a sea of online sellers, the brands that stand out are those that weave their products into the larger tapestry of their customers' lives. They're not just selling a product; they're offering an experience, an identity, a slice of a dream.

When you commit to being a true brand builder, you'll easily achieve amazing returns from your ads, gain more customers who love your brand than you thought possible, and have these customers returning repeatedly for more of what you have to offer as your revenue compounds and grows.

At this point, you might be thinking something along the lines of, *Well, I'm just a women's boutique selling clothes that, yes, I select and believe in the quality of, but creating a brand (let alone raving fans) seems like a mountain too steep to climb. I'm not funny like Chubbies or influential like Kylie. I'm just a regular guy or girl doing my thing.* You might even think that your company's appeal doesn't extend beyond the subscription you sell, the clothes you source or design, or the product you've invented and now have manufactured.

Here's where you need to shift your perspective. Every great brand starts with a simple belief in a product or an idea. What sets them apart is not just their product but their story, their authenticity, their connection with their audience, and their ability to associate that product with more pleasure and joy and less pain and suffering. That's the game.

You don't need to be famous, you don't need to be overly charismatic, and you don't need to be America's next top model to build a brand. All you need is a deep understanding of your customer and a willingness to follow a few simple frameworks that will empower you to communicate how your products can move your customers closer to their hopes, dreams, and desires and away from their pain and fears. When you get this part right, everything else will follow.

You also don't need to be world-class at running ads. You don't need to know all the technical wizardry like the back of your hand. If you are passionate about media buying and find this kind of work-life-giving, that's one thing, but as the brand founder, your time is likely better spent elsewhere. As the captain of your ship, it's your responsibility to chart the course for your brand. This involves crafting a clear and compelling vision, understanding the various elements that must be assembled to realize this vision, and vigilantly monitoring data while knowing what to look for to make informed decisions as you move forward.

In this book, you will gain insights into the mindset of an *8 Figure Owner,* discovering how to effectively deconstruct and achieve grand visions while tracking your progress along the way. You'll be equipped with specific strategies that enable you to craft compelling content and marketing tactics, laying the foundation for a brand that irresistibly draws in customers. You will also acquire practical knowledge on assembling a robust sales and marketing engine that not only generates significant revenue but establishes substantial influence and authority in your market.

As you journey forward as a brand founder, you'll notice your online store pass through different growth phases, from the initial startup and struggle to gain traction to the first signs of proof of concept and a loyal customer base and, eventually, to the various scaling phases tiered according to revenue, where your brand truly starts to flourish. Each phase comes with its own set of challenges and opportunities, and understanding them will help you navigate the ecommerce waters with greater confidence.

Typically, these growth phases align with the following monthly revenue benchmarks:

- Launch Phase: $0–$30,000 per month
- Growth Phase: $30,000–$100,000 per month
- Scaling Phase: $100,000–$1,000,000 per month
- Maturity and Expansion Phases: As the brand progresses, it enters a new phase each time its monthly revenue doubles, moving from $1 million to $2 million, then $2 million to $4 million, $4 million to $8 million, and so forth.

In each phase, there's a distinct "North Star"—a clear, overriding objective that becomes the focus until it is achieved. Moreover, each phase demands a tailored strategy, one specifically suited to the brand's current stage of growth.

If you're in the growth or scaling phase, this book is written for you. However, regardless of your current phase, remember that building an eight-figure brand is not for the faint of heart. It's certainly not for someone who desires to live a life according to the status quo. Building a brand is a marathon, not a sprint. It requires patience, resilience, critical thinking skills, and a willingness to learn and adapt.

Yet the journey of being a successful brand founder is one of the most rewarding paths a person can embark on. It offers rewards not only in terms of financial success and the admiration of friends and family but also in the deep satisfaction of creating something that genuinely adds value to your customers' lives.

Key Takeaways:

- **Branding vs. Selling:** Success hinges on building a brand, not just online selling, to stand out and safeguard against competition.

- **Reality Check:** Success in ecommerce requires more than just listing products; it's about strategic branding to avoid being undercut by larger competitors.

- **Dropshipping Caveats:** Effective dropshipping involves brand building, not just selling generic products, to create value and customer loyalty.

- **Examples of Success:** Brands like Chubbies illustrate that selling a lifestyle or experience rather than just a product fosters growth and customer loyalty.

- **Brand Building for All:** Anyone can build a brand with a deep understanding of their customers and commitment to their needs and desires.

- **Growth Phases:** Recognizing and navigating various growth phases—launch, growth, scaling, maturity—is crucial for strategic development.

- **Beyond Tactics:** Brand building transcends marketing tactics; it's about visionary leadership, data-driven decisions, and strategic adaptation.

- **Entrepreneurial Commitment:** Building a significant brand requires patience, resilience, and a dedication to adding genuine value for customers.

CHAPTER 2

Crafting Your Reality vs. Chasing Your Dreams

When I ask store owners what they want, the first answer I usually hear is "MORE." But what if there was a better alternative? What if there was an easier way to achieve your goals without the never-ending, relentless pursuit of more?

Growing up in Alaska, the only world Daniel and I knew was manual labor, specifically commercial fishing and construction. Dan started young, on the boat for weeks at a time from the age of three, and became a full-time deckhand at the age of ten. He worked in the rough waters of Kodiak, fishing for the entire summer and sometimes working up to 20 hours a day when the fishing was hot.

This makes sense, given that Dan is the son of local commercial fishing legend Tom Stafford. Tom holds the world record for the largest herring set: 1,500 tons in one scoop. With herring priced at $1,200 a ton, you can do the math and see that this one set, which took about 30 minutes to execute but a couple of days to pump and unload to the fish processors, earned him a decent amount of money.

Though I didn't start fishing until I was a young adult, both Dan and I went all in, investing hundreds of thousands of dollars to buy our operations and captain our own vessels.

We bought in because, up to this point, fishing had been awesome. It embodied a work-hard, play-hard lifestyle. We'd go out to sea for several months, hopefully make a substantial chunk of change, and then have the freedom to do fun things that young guys like to do, such as surf trips to Bali and buying motorcycles. Dan even funded and built his first home at the young age of 18. Life was fun, and since this was all either of us had ever really known, we bit the bullet and set our lives on this trajectory.

The problem was that as soon as we both got married and started having our own children, heading out to sea for months at a time became much less fun. It was awful, actually. We were pretty good at fishing and very hard workers, so financially, we were always able to provide, even in seasons when others would struggle. Commercial fishing is highly competitive and risky; if the fish show up and you catch them first, despite dozens of others trying to outwork and outsmart you, and if the canneries are willing to pay a good price for those fish, then and only then do you make money. If any of those things don't happen, you don't.

One September night, on my smaller, 30-foot boat, when I really just wanted to go home (I had been fishing since May when the salmon season opened), I looked across the pitch-black, stormy waters and sideways rain and saw a salty old man working his gear. He was alone, and it was clear that he had been drinking. At that moment, I realized that if I didn't change my trajectory, that would be me one day. I also realized that I had been gone for four of the seven months of my first-born daughter Eleanor's life. I admit this thought is dramatic, but the realization that I had been gone for over half of her life really disturbed me. I decided to call it quits and head in for the season the next day.

Earlier that same summer, Dan had been captaining his larger fishing boat, which required the help of three other crewmen, unlike my smaller operation, which needed just me and one other guy. Dan's wife, Sammy, who was nine months pregnant, traveled to Valdez for a visit. She was journeying from town with Dan's dad, who was making a quick stop for supplies, to spend a few days with Dan on the boat before giving birth to their first son.

As the weather worsened, Dan began tanking down his fish hold (a cavity in the center of the boat large enough to contain 40,000 pounds of salmon) to stabilize the boat in the rising weather. The fish hold was about halfway full when a rogue wave hit the side of the boat. When the hold is only half full, water can slosh to the side and roll the boat over, which is exactly what happened.

Dan, at the helm on the uphill side, quickly climbed out of the driver's window and scurried along the boat as it flipped completely upside down. Somehow, he managed to keep his phone safe and dry in his pocket. He immediately called for help and then began problem-solving how to get the other crew members out and prevent them from drowning.

Three others were trapped inside the cabin, as water pressure held all the doors shut, and water was rushing in through the open windows, filling the cabin. Despite their efforts, they couldn't break a door or window to escape. They took one last breath before the cabin was completely filled, and when it did, the pressure decreased just enough to allow the door to be kicked open. Still, the water rushing in was so intense that it actually ripped the pants off one of the crew members trying to escape.

Though they had hope, they were not out of danger yet. Having escaped the boat, they now had to navigate through the dumped fishing net and fight their way to the surface. One by one, the crew members emerged, and Dan helped them onto the small, still-floating part of the boat. Shortly after, Tom arrived and brought all the crew members back to safety.

Dan's boat was greatly underinsured. In a single moment, he'd lost everything: his savings, his equity, and his desire to ever fish again. He felt like a complete failure. This incident kickstarted a several-year battle with PTSD for Dan, his family, and the crew.

But life doesn't pause for traumatic events. Days after this happened, Sammy went into labor. Dan was faced with the challenge of trying to be present for the birth of his child despite the intensity of his situation. He often woke up with night terrors and would run to the windows because he thought the building he was sleeping in was rolling and sinking. He also had to figure out how to provide for his family despite spending everything they had without catching a season's worth of fish. He would have to return to sea with a leased boat to salvage what he could from the season.

Why is This Important?

So, what does all this have to do with ecommerce and building a reality that you love? Trust me, there's a point to this story.

Once the dust settled, Dan and I had a chance to zoom out and consider the trajectory of our lives. Like many people, we had just been doing what we always knew. However, we both knew there had to be a better way to make money, one that would allow us to be closer to our families, prioritize our health, and actually enjoy our lives and our summers rather than tirelessly working on a boat for a few dollars.

We began to believe we could make not just enough money to comfortably get by but to actually become wealthy. For us, wealth meant less chaos and more order, physical and mental health, and prosperity in every aspect of our lives. We wanted every part of our lives—body, soul, spirit, relationships, dreams, and work—to be nourished, growing, and thriving.

Dan had read the book *Think and Grow Rich* by Napoleon Hill, and he shared it with me. This was a huge shift for us because, for the first time in our lives, we believed all of this could be possible. We learned that success begins with a strong desire, faith, and persistence. Furthermore, when these are combined with a clear plan and a positive mental attitude, we believe we can turn dreams into reality.

Most of the time, being out on the water was adventurous and fun, and we were always documenting the crazy adventures we had as fishermen, from surfing with sea lions to jumping off icebergs. Since many business owners had asked if we could make videos to promote their businesses, we started a production company built around our passion for making videos. However, like many entrepreneurial journeys, we initially missed the mark.

Our clients loved the videos we produced for them, but when we asked if the videos had positively impacted their business, the short answer was no. This deeply bothered us, but it forced us to answer the question, "What should a business do with a good promotional video to grow its sales?" We joined masterminds and hired coaches, and gradually, we shifted our focus from video production to marketing, specifically for ecommerce brands.

We've now worked with over four hundred stores and helped generate hundreds of millions of dollars for our clients. This is very humbling, considering that at one point, we were just two young commercial fishermen from a small town of five thousand in Southcentral Alaska.

"Okay Robby, Get to the Point!"

So, again, what does this have to do with you and accomplishing your vision?

When it comes to setting a vision for their business, although the details often appear less extreme, most people follow a path very similar to the one Dan and I took. First, they realize that the trajectory they're on isn't leading them to where they want to end up. Then, they choose to pursue something they are passionate about that has a realistic chance of making money. After that, they simply try as hard as they can to increase their earnings.

When we started the video production company, Dan and I thought that if we could make $25,000 a month, we would be set for life. The idea was that we could each take home $10,000 and have an extra $5,000 to reinvest in the business and cover any expenses. Looking back, the naivety of this plan is cringe-worthy, and we have since learned much more about how much money it takes to run a legitimate business.

Financially speaking, the first year we focused on video production was pretty horrific. We made some money, but after paying the bills, there was rarely anything left to bring home to our families. The feelings of being foolish and failures and the shame of quitting something that, though difficult and dangerous, at least provided for our families intensified.

My wife would often graciously ask, "Do you think we'll be able to pay ourselves anything this month?" Each time, I would stumble through my words, saying that there wasn't enough money to pay ourselves but that I thought it would be worth it someday and she could trust me. I barely trusted myself and had no idea whether or not this would work out. Dan and I would often take on the occasional fishing trip or construction project to get by, but as time went on, our hearts became less and less interested in it.

Thankfully, after a year of struggle and finding our niche in ecommerce, we quickly reached the $25k-per-month milestone in the early days of year two. Like most people, we then expanded our vision to $50k per month. This expansion was necessary because any legitimate business owner knows that taking home 80% of the gross revenue is not sustainable in a fully functional business with real expenses. We soon hit our goal of $50k and asked ourselves, *What should we do next?* We proceeded to double our goals over and over again until, one day, we broke the whole business.

A mentor of mine once said, "The only way to figure out how fast and how far you can run is to run as fast as you can until you fall over and die."

Five years into our business, by following the wins and always choosing the path of least resistance, we had scaled into something indistinguishable from where we had started. That isn't all bad, right? We'd been blessed to learn a lot and help many people along the way, but we went too far too fast and built something that we didn't even know was prone to fall. And fall we did, a great story that will be shared later in the book.

Most people choose something they enjoy that has the potential for wealth and start aiming for more. Once they attain more, they decide to go for even greater amounts. Eventually, those who become skilled at getting more continue to do so until they crash and burn.

Ecological philosopher Edward Abbey once declared, "Growth for the sake of growth is the ideology of the cancer cell."

Now, don't get me wrong. My life revolves around living boldly and empowering myself and others in the joyous, relentless pursuit of big visions. But what if there were a better, more effective way to achieve your dreams than constantly trying to aim for "more"?

The Problems with Solving for More

Unhealthy Growth: Growth for the sake of growth isn't always healthy or beneficial. Just ask the CEO of any successful company. Instead, our focus should be on serving our market better and becoming so good at what we do that not growing would be a disservice to humanity. Truett Cathy, former CEO of Chick-fil-A, put it this way: "If we get better, our customers will demand that we get bigger." This is much different from doing whatever it takes to hit your next number and leaving a pile of bad experiences and poor customer reviews in your wake because you went too fast and lost focus on the people, purpose, and impact.

No Clarity: A company's vision is meant to provide clear direction to its people. It should be so illuminating that it highlights the values and philosophies leaders ought to consider when making decisions and steer their involvement toward the crystal-clear picture painted by the vision. When you're simply solving for "more," there are an infinite number of ways to get there because "more" could be anything.

Everybody loves making more money, but very few understand how easy it is to lose traction, get stuck on a plateau, and begin deteriorating because you've tried to get more without putting much thought into how the pieces fit together. Achieving healthy growth requires a high degree of clarity and intentionality.

It's about aligning and compounding various growth strategies in a holistic manner that benefits the business as a whole.

Closer: A Much Better Alternative to "More"

Instead of pursuing every opportunity that comes your way with little regard for the full implications, what I'd like to propose is that you only say yes to opportunities that bring you closer to your desired outcome.

This is easier said than done for a number of reasons. Here are two. First, this requires that you get clear on what it is that you actually want. Second, by creating a crystal-clear definition of what success looks like, you are simultaneously defining failure, and most people avoid failure at all costs because it sucks and is painful. Often, people prefer to have a vague idea of what success should look like. They try to keep a happy-go-lucky attitude so they never have to feel like they've missed the mark.

Start With the End in Mind

To move away from the risky game of unchecked growth at all costs and transition into deliberate, purposeful, and efficient growth, we must start with the end in mind, isolate the variables, set our trajectory, and let time do its work.

Imagine having your own business GPS. When you know your destination, reverse engineering the steps to get there becomes a straightforward task. It's like plugging an address into Google Maps. Without a destination, you're lost in a sea of options, much like being dropped in the middle of a bustling city with no idea of where to go. It's overwhelming, frustrating, and a recipe for getting nowhere fast. But with a destination punched in, Google Maps doesn't just give you a route; it gives you the best route. Suddenly, a once-daunting journey is broken down into manageable, step-by-step instructions. It even gives an ETA.

This principle is crucial in the business world. Knowing your end goal gives you a clear path to follow. It means you can focus your energy on what's important, streamline your efforts, and avoid getting sidetracked by distractions that don't serve your ultimate objective. It's about efficiency and effectiveness, about not just moving but moving in the right direction in the least amount of time possible.

It's also about not overshooting your goals, avoiding the mistake of walking past a wonderful life that's already available to you, and not entering into a world you never wanted for yourself, which almost always leads to self-destruction.

Here is a simple example of what "starting with the end in mind" could look like:

Three years from now, my company will consistently generate $1,000,000 per month in gross revenue with an 18% net profit. This will enable me to hire world-class professionals to oversee operations and manage the aspects of the company where my expertise isn't the strongest. This, in turn, allows me to focus on the areas that truly ignite my passion, such as new product development and creating social content. My customers will frequently provide unsolicited five-star reviews, and word-of-mouth recommendations about our products will spread rapidly. Many influencers will be eager to share their love for our products, occasionally leading to significant sales spikes when their endorsements go viral.

The success of my company will afford me a salary of $25,000 per month, enabling me to fund the lifestyle of my dreams. I will work 25 hours a week only on things that I love. I will have the ability to save money, invest wisely, and donate generously from my monthly income. Additionally, I plan to build the house I've always wanted and take my family on fantastic vacations every three to four months. As time progresses, the value of my company will increase, and we will build substantial cash reserves to comfortably navigate slower business periods. While I anticipate receiving numerous offers to buy the company, I will patiently wait for the right one, as I am not in a rush to exit a business that I deeply love and enjoy.

Isolate the Variables

Once you have a clear destination for where you want to take your business and how that will impact you personally, you need to isolate three important variables to crystallize a plan that informs what you do on a daily, monthly, quarterly, and annual basis: pinpoint your current location, define your desired destination, and determine how quickly you want to get there. These variables are the building blocks of an actionable plan that will guide your every move.

Google Maps can't give you a route to your destination without first knowing where you are, and similarly, you can't chart a path forward without an accurate picture of where you are, including your strengths, weaknesses, opportunities, and threats. Self-awareness is crucial. It enables you to take stock of your resources, understand your limitations, and identify the areas that require your immediate attention.

Next, you must have a vision of where you want to be. This isn't just about setting lofty revenue goals or dreaming of market dominance. It's about understanding what success looks like in the most concrete terms, be it ideal lifestyle, market share, customer satisfaction, or brand reputation.

Finally, when it comes to creating an action plan that informs your behavior, the speed at which you aim to reach your goal is important. For instance, the actions you take to arrive at your destination in just one year may differ significantly from those you would take if you allowed yourself five years. A one-year plan might require you to find partners and raise outside investment capital to aggressively market your business. In contrast, a five-year plan could involve a self-funded approach, where you increase ad spend by 10% per quarter using incoming sales revenue.

By isolating these variables, you transform a once vague and daunting goal into a series of precise, manageable steps, with waypoints along the way, each marking a significant milestone toward your ultimate destination.

Remember, small, compounding wins lead to big victories. The beauty of this approach is that each step, no matter how small, builds upon the last. Over time, these incremental gains accumulate, propelling you toward your goal faster than you might expect. It's a strategy where you can confidently celebrate even the smallest victories and use them as fuel for your journey because you know you are making undeniable progress. One day, you'll look up and realize that you are much closer to your desired outcome than you thought.

In the end, isolating the variables isn't just about plotting a course; it's about moving forward with clarity and confidence, knowing that every step you take is a calculated move toward a future you've envisioned and a destiny you've chosen.

At one point in my journey, I felt as though the goals I had set were holding a gun to my head. No matter how hard I tried, I couldn't seem to hit them. Having large goals tormented me. The secret, I discovered, lay in a simple yet powerful shift in perspective. I had to understand that I didn't actually need my goals to happen.

When you're motivated out of need, you act out of desperation, fill your head with anxiety, and make poor decisions. Instead, I made the powerful choice to pursue large and lofty goals not because I needed to but simply because I wanted to. At the end of the day, I knew I could easily and sufficiently provide for my family and not just meet all of their basic needs but do so abundantly. So, why was I so stressed out? After this shift, I became way less driven by anxiety and irrational fear and more by enjoyment, creativity, and impact.

A Final Word on Building Your Reality vs. Chasing Your Dreams

When Dan and I transitioned from the commercial fishing industry to something more aligned with our life goals, we were determined not to replicate the toxic environment we were leaving behind. Early on, we established a principle of "non-negotiables" to ensure a healthy work-life balance.

For instance, we committed to being home for dinner by 5:00 PM, regardless of how much work there was to be done. Given our past, this time constraint was actually quite difficult for us. We were always "do it till it's done" kind of guys, but it forced a level of efficiency and innovation that we would have never discovered had we allowed for unlimited working hours. We also carved out time for daily exercise. These non-negotiables were crucial in preventing our goals from consuming our lives and creating a reality we didn't want to live in.

However, as our business grew, we overlooked the need to be adaptable and update these non-negotiables as seasons changed. This oversight led to scaling into something we didn't want and resulted in a significant downturn that could have been avoided. My advice to you as you set your vision is to define clear boundaries around what you're not willing to sacrifice. That way, as your business progresses and becomes successful, your personal life will improve in tandem with it rather than becoming a source of stress. Success in business shouldn't come at the cost of your well-being or your family's happiness.

Key Takeaways:

- **Importance of Vision:** Establishing a clear vision for the future is crucial. Without it, efforts can be misdirected, and opportunities for true fulfillment and success can be missed.

- **Setting Clear Goals:** Defining success in concrete terms helps create a roadmap to achieve it, emphasizing the necessity of knowing both the starting point and the desired destination.

- **Isolating Variables for Planning:** Identifying where you are, where you want to be, and how fast you want to get there is essential for developing an actionable plan that guides daily actions.

- **Small Wins Matter:** Appreciating incremental progress is important. Small, compounding wins over time can lead to significant achievements.

- **Work-Life Balance:** Establishing "non-negotiables" for personal time and health is vital. Success should not come at the expense of personal well-being.

- **Adapting Non-Negotiables:** As circumstances change, so should your non-negotiables to ensure they continue to support your overall well-being and happiness alongside business growth.

CHAPTER 3

Engineering Success: Calculating Realistic Moves Instead of Hoping for 10x

What if there was a way to profitably grow your revenue and leave your competition in the dust even if you're not currently hitting your return on ad spend (ROAS) target?

Many people have performance targets, and whether or not they hit them often comes down to which of the two strategies they used. The first involves investing heavily in ads and scaling up as much as possible before falling below the target. The second adopts a more conservative approach, maintaining a minimum baseline budget to test new ideas until the target is met or exceeded, at which point the brand feels comfortable scaling again. It's your classic "If we're above 6x, spend as much as you can; if not, let's return to the drawing board and continue testing" conversation.

Setting performance targets is a fairly simple process for most people. They begin by tabulating the variable costs associated with preparing their product for sale and adding the cost of shipping, taxes, etc. Then they see what's left over and make a reasonable estimate of how much they can afford to spend on marketing to generate a sale while still retaining some profit, all while keeping a vague idea of fixed costs, things like rent and labor, in the back of their head.

They also take into account the previous success of their ads, blending this information with a mix of gut feelings and hard numbers. From this, they determine a target ROAS necessary for success, around which they plan their entire business, and they seldom revisit or question this target. They simply feel like they know that this is what is required for their business to work. I've seen this number be as high as 12x and as low as 0.5x.

This approach might seem logical, right? Well, it's not. In fact, it's a terrible way to set your targets. If you've been doing it this way, you're likely leaving a significant amount of money on the table. In fact, you might be in a position to double your annual sales profitably this year without increasing the performance of your marketing at all.

We need to grasp a few concepts to understand why this is a poor approach to setting targets, which act as a governor for your growth by indicating when you can and cannot scale, and to learn how to develop a better navigation system for capturing market share and accumulating profits.

First, when an ad platform uses the word "auction" to describe what's happening behind the scenes with their algorithm, what does that mean? Is it literally an auction, or is it just fancy language? Second, ROAS is not the same as profit. And third, the first purchase is only half the story.

Ad Auctions Explained

Every time there's a chance to show your ad to someone in your audience across ad platforms like Facebook, Instagram, and TikTok, it enters an ad auction to determine who should see it. The goal of an auction is simple: to pair your ad with people in your audience who are most likely to be interested in it.

Ad platforms structure the auction this way to help you get the most results possible for your budget while providing a positive, relevant experience for their users.

While traditional auctions pick a winner based on the highest bid, ad auctions consider several factors to determine which ad is displayed.

Ads that perform best combine five components: the right objective, targeting, a sufficient budget, enough duration, and compelling ad creative.

Instead of boring you with a detailed explanation of each of these components, I will get right to the point. Your biggest levers when it comes to beating out the competition and scaling your revenue are the creative and the budget.

As ad platforms introduce more machine learning and AI into their algorithms, the competitive edge people get from pushing all the right buttons at the right time will continue to go down. This means that soon, everybody is going to be a world-class media buyer because everything is literally going to be automated. We're not quite there yet, but we're moving in that direction quickly.

The difference between brands that are scaling to the moon and the ones that are meandering around is how persuasive their ads are and how much they are willing to spend to acquire a customer.

Zuckerburg can use whatever fancy language he wants, but at the end of the day, if you're willing to spend and you master the art of ad creative, your experience with ads can and should be viewed like a literal auction where the highest bidder wins. This leads me to my next point: if this is truly the case, then using

ROAS to determine when you should scale no longer makes any sense.

ROAS is Not Profit

Although we love getting sky-high returns and do it all the time, getting to a million dollars a month and beyond is not achieved by maintaining 10x ROAS. It is achieved from sales velocity, from taking market share and acquiring tons of customers. This is why we do marketing: to get more customers. The problem with having a ROAS target as your primary guide is that it will often tell you to stop marketing. Meanwhile, people who understand how the game is played will double down and leave you in the dust.

It is a fact that when you spend more, at some point, your ROAS will start to go down. When faced with the dilemma of diminishing returns, you have two options: pull back and spend or continue spending despite ROAS going down.

Most people choose the first option. In reverence to their ROAS target, they rip apart everything that brought them to their current position. They restructure the campaigns, launch new offers, and build new ad creatives, all without realizing that they've just firmly planted their feet onto a plateau and chosen less profit, which means fewer dollars in their pocket.

Would you prefer to spend $800 a day to acquire 84 customers at a 7.9x return, resulting in a total of $6,315 in revenue and $564 in daily profit, or spend $2,500 a day to acquire 124 customers at a 3.7x return, resulting in a total of $9,243 in revenue and $826 in daily profit?

And what sounds harder, maintaining a 7.9x return or maintaining a 3.7x return?

Obviously, once you do the math, anyone in their right mind will choose more money and easier-to-hit targets.

So, what's the catch? You just have to be willing to spend more. That's it. And here's the thing: you can easily work your way up to this. Creating the cash necessary for more ad spend is actually pretty easy once you have the plan and take into consideration the inevitable fact that returns will diminish as spending increases.

This realization has unlocked immediate scaling opportunities for numerous brands: achieving higher customer volumes, even with a decreased ROAS, is more profitable than relying solely on an extremely high ROAS with limited customer volume. It's helped many people go from feeling like they can never make things work to getting results they've only dreamt about. But that's not even the best part.

The First Purchase Is Only Half the Story

Now that we understand that the highest bidder wins (which literally means the person willing to have the lowest ROAS wins) and that having more customers is much more profitable than having a high ROAS, let's go back to the two scenarios we ran earlier and check out the compounding growth that takes place as a percentage of the new customers purchase again.

Scenario one involved spending $800 a day to acquire 84 customers at a 7.9x return, resulting in a total of $6,315 in revenue and $564 in daily profit.

When multiplied by 365 days for the year, we get the following numbers:

Spend: $292,000
ROAS: 7.9
New Customers: 30,660
Revenue: $2,304,975
Profit: $205,860

When 30% of the new customers, amounting to 9,198 people, purchase again throughout the year, $691,505.64 will be added to the total revenue without any additional ad spend, bringing the total revenue up to $2,996,480.64. Once the cost of goods sold (COGS) is factored in, profit increases from $205,860 to $477,138.

Amazing, right? Just wait until you see scenario two.

In scenario two, we spend $2,500 a day to acquire 124 customers at a 3.7x return, resulting in a total of $9,243 in revenue and $826 in daily profit.

When multiplied by 365 days for the year, we get the following numbers:

Spend: $912,500
ROAS: 3.7
New Customers: 45,260
Revenue: $3,373,695
Profit: $301,490

When 30% of the new customers, which is 13,578 people, purchase again throughout the year, an additional $1,020,794.04 is added to the total revenue without any additional ad spend, bringing total revenue up to $4,394,489.04 and profit from $301,490 to $617,936.15!

Put simply, the person who was happy with a 3.7x return brought home $618k in profit and acquired 45,000 customers, while the one who aimed to maintain a 7.9x return only brought in $477k in profit with 30,000 customers. Which one do you want to be?

Building a Foundation That Scales

Sadly, in the direct-to-consumer world, some brands really do need to achieve a 10x return to survive because their business infrastructure doesn't allow for anything less. If you sell a product that costs only $9.99 and you churn through customers like crazy, you will never be able to scale your marketing efforts. Acquiring new customers for ten dollars or less isn't realistic at scale, and without a growing customer base, your business will eventually wither and die. To make sure this isn't you, I've detailed five foundational pillars every brand must strive to meet to position themselves for explosive revenue growth.

1. The product you're selling should have gross margins of 60-70% or more. If it doesn't, you're never really going to be able to scale hard because there's simply not enough margin to cover your customer acquisition costs.

2. Your average order value (AOV) should be over $70 so the net dollar amount is high enough to cover your customer acquisition cost (CAC).

3. Your product needs to have a healthy repeat purchase rate, or you must have an AOV of over $400 to make up for the lack of LTV that comes from repeat purchases.

4. There needs to be something unique about the product, and you need a good brand story so you have something powerful to leverage across your advertising efforts.

And lastly…

5. Your products need to be great so the reviews are strong and the word of mouth grows as you scale.

We love guiding principles because they steer us toward success. But if reading these five pillars just gave you a mini-heart attack, don't worry -- it means you've come to the right place. Throughout this book, you will not only learn what it takes to position yourself for success, but you'll also discover strategies and tactics to improve aspects like your AOV if it's currently not where it needs to be.

North Star Metrics (How to Monitor Progress)

In Chapter 2, we discussed achieving our goals as efficiently as possible. We used the example of Google Maps to illustrate that focusing on all the side roads instead of a direct path to your destination could prevent you from arriving or at least slow you down.

The same concept applies when looking at performance data to scale your revenue. More data doesn't necessarily mean more money. It's actually the proper use of data to make the right decisions that matters. Personally, I couldn't care less about this attribution model versus that one and all the technical jargon. I just want to ensure we're meeting our goals and making money.

If you don't know what your North Star metrics are, you're wandering down side roads when you should be on the direct route with Google Maps. Below are the metrics you should be looking at regularly to make sure you're on the right path.

- **Blended ROAS (Return on Ad Spend):** Evaluates the overall return from your advertising investments across all channels combined. It's essential for ensuring your marketing efforts are generating more revenue than the costs incurred.

- **MER (Marketing Efficiency Ratio):** Indicates the total revenue generated for every dollar spent on marketing as a percentage, highlighting the efficiency of your marketing budget.

- **Blended Ad Spend:** The aggregate advertising expenditure across all platforms crucial for managing costs and optimizing marketing budget allocation.

- **NCAC (Cost to Acquire a New Customer):** Reflects the expense involved in acquiring a new customer. Tracking this helps you understand the investment needed to expand your customer base.

- **Sales:** The total revenue from sold products, a fundamental measure of your business's financial health and growth.

- **Orders:** The count of orders placed, offering insights into transaction volumes and customer demand.

- **AOV (Average Order Value):** The average spending per order, key for strategies aimed at boosting transactional revenue.

- **CPA (Cost Per Acquisition or Purchase):** The cost to generate a purchase, considering both new and existing customers. Monitoring CPA is crucial for evaluating the efficiency of marketing efforts in driving not just new business but overall sales.

- **New Customers:** The number of customers making their first purchase within a specific period, important for assessing customer base growth and acquisition strategy success.

- **Returning Customers:** The number of repeat purchasers which is vital for measuring customer loyalty and the effectiveness of retention strategies.

- **LTV/CPA (Lifetime Value to Cost Per Acquisition Ratio):** Comparison of the total value a customer contributes over their lifetime to the cost of acquiring them, highlighting the long-term profitability of customer relationships.

- **Sessions:** The total interactions with your website in a given timeframe, an indicator of user engagement and potential conversion opportunities.

- **Conversion Rate:** The ratio of sessions that result in a sale, crucial for gauging the success of your website and marketing in converting visitors into buyers.

By regularly monitoring these metrics, you equip your business with a compass to navigate the complexities of growth and competition. These indicators serve as benchmarks for assessing performance, optimizing strategies, and ensuring that your business follows the most direct and efficient path to success.

Numerous methods and tools are available for compiling and analyzing this data. We prefer to automate this process with a tool called Triple Whale, which allows us to easily create a dashboard of our North Star metrics. That way, we can view performance data at a glance and then delve deeper into individual platforms and more granular metrics, such as the specific click-through rate of a particular ad, on an as-needed basis.

With an understanding of how to set performance targets that prioritize growing your customer base and profit above arbitrary ROAS goals, along with a clear picture of the foundational pillars necessary for scaling and a list of numbers to ensure you're moving in the right direction, you're going to be miles ahead of the competition. When in doubt, remember this: whoever is willing to spend the most to acquire a customer and outbid their competition wins.

So, can you really get more customers and make more profit with easier targets? Yes. If you follow the upcoming strategies and ensure your marketing strategy is solid, without major gaps that could drastically lower your performance due to missing pieces or complete negligence, that's exactly what I'm suggesting, and we've been blessed to partner with many people who've done so.

Key Takeaways:

- **Beyond ROAS Targets:** Setting realistic performance targets is crucial. Overshooting or undershooting ROAS targets can either leave money on the table or hinder growth.

- **Understanding Ad Auctions:** Ad auctions on platforms like Facebook and Instagram prioritize creative quality and budget, highlighting the importance of persuasive ads and willingness to spend for customer acquisition.

- **ROAS Misconceptions:** Aiming for high ROAS can limit growth. Brands that accept lower ROAS while focusing on sales velocity and market share can profit more by acquiring more customers.

- **Comprehensive Growth Strategy:** Growth involves more than just initial purchases; considering repeat customers and their lifetime value is essential for sustainable expansion.

- **Foundational Pillars for Scaling:** Success factors include having a high gross margin (70%+), an AOV over $70, a unique product with a compelling brand story, and excellent product quality to foster customer loyalty and repeat business.

- **North Star Metrics**: Key metrics for guiding business decisions include blended ROAS, marketing efficiency ratio (MER), new customer acquisition cost (NCAC), and lifetime value to cost per acquisition ratio (LTV/CPA).

- **Efficient Use of Data:** Regular monitoring of essential metrics ensures businesses stay on the path to achieving their goals without getting lost in less relevant data.

CHAPTER 4

Rich Brand, Poor Brand: Achieving Real Wealth in Ecommerce

This chapter is for the person who wakes up most days ready to conquer the world, bright-eyed and bushy-tailed, eager to kick some ass, but who, on rare occasions during those dark and dreary days that inevitably come from time to time, finds themselves haunted with one or more of the following fleeting thoughts:

- *What if all my efforts amount to nothing more than a big waste of time?*

- *What if I'm just a few short months of poor performance away from everything collapsing, leaving me with nothing but a mountain of debt and inventory?*

- *What if I give this my all, investing as much time and energy as possible, and it still doesn't get me where I want to go?*

If that's you, then you're in good company. In fact, most people have days where they question the value of what they're building, myself included. Unfortunately, most brand founders have good reason to wonder.

But what if these doubts were nothing but nasty little lies from the pit of hell? What if what you're building is actually more valuable than you thought, both in its capacity to positively impact the world and generate real wealth for you? What if you're only a few small tweaks from not just thinking positively about the strength of your store but experiencing undeniable evidence of its value?

Over the years, I've seen brands fall into two categories. On the surface, they look very similar, but under the hood, they are vastly different. One is a rich brand, and the other is a poor brand. Oddly enough, it's not their revenue that determines which category they fall into.

Let's start with the poor brand. There are two types of poor brands: ones that are over-reliant on ads and ones that achieve limited success without ads and don't understand how to use them as a tool to reach new heights.

Poor Brands With an Over-Reliance on Ads

These brands start with an exciting vision of the future, where products fly off the shelves, selling at a premium price, and they are admired by their customers and feared by their competitors. Over time, as the vision begins to materialize and makes its way to the starting line, the brand gets slowly chiseled down and becomes less and less magnificent.

The brass tacks of real life repeatedly butt their heads in, and by the time the products have been manufactured or sourced, they are slightly less magnificent than what the founder originally dreamed of but are still good enough to get started. The brand usually figures that this can be improved once they have some momentum, but they just need to get started.

So, with a plan and a product, the brand launches, and people actually begin buying—amazing! The brand successfully picks up a small army of support from friends, family, and the local community, but it soon becomes obvious that to go beyond these circles, something needs to change. It's the same people liking and commenting on the posts, most of whom have already bought products and shared their support.

Ads are the logical next step, so they learn the basics, launch some ads, and start reaching people who were previously unreachable. It's like magic; they're sending out more orders than ever, and their customer base is growing, so they double down.

Excited by the growth and ready to take on the world, they begin hiring and making investments in the business. They hire help for customer service and social media, bring on staff for fulfilling orders, secure a little bookkeeping assistance, invest in new product lines, embark on new marketing initiatives, and maybe even acquire a legitimate workspace that doubles as a content studio and warehouse.

Life is great, but then the ads stop working as well as they once did, and sales dip. They realize that all their new expenses, though necessary to run the now larger business, are going to bleed them dry if sales don't get back on track, leading to their first "oh, shit" moment. Dependent on all these new enhancements, the brand scales back where it can, starting with ad spend. They conclude that they must stop the bleeding and get their performance back on track.

In doing so, they save some short-term cash but fail to realize that the problem will only worsen because, with lower ad spend, they are acquiring fewer customers. Now, instead of having a growing client base, it has begun to diminish, along with the revenue from repeat purchases of existing customers.

Soon, the brand faces their second "oh, shit" moment and begins cutting expenses and searching for a silver-bullet marketing solution, only to realize that all the marketing help they've received from agencies, gurus, and experts is, at best, only marginally better than what they were doing previously, and their desperation grows. The brand that was once booming and easily growing is now desperate for ad performance as their saving grace.

Poor Brands with Organic Growth and a Failure to Implement the Use of Ads?

Similar to the brand that ends up in a tricky situation due to an over-reliance on ads, this poor brand also has a vision of the future, but its vision emerges after some success online. Perhaps they launched something like a clothing boutique and made a surprising number of sales, getting a glimpse of their potential. Their first "oh, shit" moment is actually an exciting one, like "Oh, shit—this could be huge."

But instead of immediately hitting a plateau after exhausting the audience of friends, family, and close circles, they continue building momentum for a while. This brand has tapped into the power of building and hosting an online community, effectively drawing more and more people in. Maybe it's a social media movement behind a product designed to solve a specific issue (for example, a swimsuit that is flattering but not exploitative), or perhaps it's a fun Facebook group where moms share the pain of literally not having the time to find new clothes for bodies that are indistinguishable from the ones they once had.

Not only has the brand provided a community of new friends, but it has also provided an easy way to shop from home through live streams. These streams always have new, cute clothes that actually fit and are affordable.

To continue growing, this brand makes the mistake of believing that they must simply do more. So they do more photoshoots, more Instagram or TikTok stories, more posts, more product lines, more live streams, more sale events, and more new product drops, all of which are dependent on the efforts of the founder. But one day, they start to waver.

Whether it was through an ad they saw, a friend they heard from, or simply through observation, they realized that ads could be a helpful tool for continued growth. Ads might even help them win back some of their time and become less dependent on the unsustainable number of hours they are putting into the business, all while juggling family life.

Recognizing their limitations, they decide to outsource their advertising efforts, aiming to change their company's direction. However, after several months of hopeful attempts, they face some harsh realities.

First, the campaigns managed by their new advertising specialist feel disconnected, failing to capture the essence of the authentic content that initially fueled the brand's success. Second, despite receiving assurances of impressive results, the brand observes no significant impact on sales. Finally, the financial strain of the advertising specialist's fees combined with the ad spend becomes increasingly difficult to justify, especially with the negligible uptick in sales.

This series of disappointments leads to a sobering conclusion: they are back to square one, overwhelmed and stagnant, with all their effort and investment feeling like a big waste of time.

Man, that's depressing. The good news is that most rich brands have had some version of the poor brand in their past, which inspired their pivot into real wealth. So, if any of that feels familiar, just know you're doing exactly what you need to be doing and on the right path.

Let's contrast the poor brand with the rich brand. The differences can seem subtle in action if you don't know what you're looking for, but they're monumental in where they end up.

Rich Brand

Rather than being obsessed with today's performance, rich brands are on a mission and have a dream that goes beyond immediate success. They aim for a grand finale that generates substantial wealth for the founder through building and selling their brand or creating a sustainable revenue stream that gets directed towards investments that will compound over time. This approach involves reverse engineering from a desired outcome and considers crafting a lifestyle and legacy rather than mere sales.

As highlighted by business coach Dan Sullivan, true wealth includes not just financial freedom but also the freedom of time, relationships, and purpose.

Let's talk about financial freedom first, starting with brands that build and sell.

Rich Brands That Build and Sell:

When an exit is the end goal, your approach to growth changes significantly. Founders who choose this path often employ a strategy that involves working backward from the exit goal to tell a story that enhances the brand's value and commands a higher selling price.

So, what does "telling a story that commands a higher selling price" at the time of sale look like? Here are eight key observations of the practices that rich brands have locked in, while poor brands are sacrificing anything and everything they can on the altar of growth.

1. **A Solid AOV to LTV Ratio:** This reflects a healthy balance between the average amount a customer spends per order (AOV) and the total amount they spend over their entire relationship with the store (LTV). This ratio is crucial for understanding customer value and profitability.

   A solid AOV to LTV ratio indicates that a business is not only successful in securing initial sales but is also effective in retaining customers and encouraging them to make more valuable purchases over time. While the ideal ratio can vary depending on the business model, industry, and margins, a higher LTV compared to AOV is what you're looking for. It suggests that customers continue to purchase after their initial order, indicating strong customer loyalty and a successful long-term business strategy.

   There's no one-size-fits-all answer for what constitutes a "solid" AOV to LTV ratio, as it highly depends on the specific costs and margins of the products being sold. However, a general benchmark for many ecommerce businesses is to aim for an LTV that is 3x the AOV. This indicates that the average customer is generating profit well beyond their initial purchase, helping to cover the costs of acquisition and operations while still leaving room for profit.

Companies lacking a solid average order value to lifetime value ratio rely too much on front-end acquisition. This approach is kind of like kicking the can down the road, putting them at risk. If the ad account gets shut down, the business will soon follow if that is solely what the brand relies on.

2. **A Strong Brand:** Having a strong brand means possessing a distinct and compelling identity that resonates deeply with your customers, fostering loyalty and differentiating the brand in the marketplace. This is such a big topic that we will spend the entirety of the next chapter deconstructing the process of building a strong brand.

3. **Customer Acquisition:** Rich brands have figured out how to consistently acquire customers within a clearly defined and heavily monitored CAC (cost to acquire a customer) threshold while continuously testing new approaches to combat ad fatigue and diminishing returns.

4. **Stay Lean:** Rich brands keep G&A (general and administrative) expenses below 20% of their revenue. G&A refers to a company's operating expenses that remain constant regardless of sales or production levels. G&A expenses include building expenses, salaries and wages, insurance, licenses, fees, and supplies.

5. **Build Cash Reserves:** It is generally recommended that you aim for a minimum cash reserve equivalent to three months of fixed expenses. Achieving a six-month cushion empowers you to confidently pursue more ambitious risks with higher rewards.

6. **Make Decisions Based on Customer Feedback:** Actively seek and analyze feedback from your customers to better understand their desires and needs. Use this insight to identify potential gaps in your offerings and explore opportunities for ancillary products. Aligning product development and service enhancements with customer feedback not only meets their current needs but also anticipates future demands. This fosters a deeper connection and enhances customer satisfaction, ensuring your brand remains relevant and continues to evolve in alignment with your customers' preferences, driving sustained growth and loyalty.

7. **Maintain Visionary Leadership:** It's absolutely crucial for the founder to consistently champion and uphold the long-term vision of the company, steering clear of getting caught in the weeds of daily operations. This requires the ability to constantly zoom in and out of everyday decisions to ensure they align with the big-picture goals and future direction of the business.

By delegating day-to-day tasks to trusted team members, the founder can dedicate their energy to strategic planning, innovation, and growth initiatives that propel the company forward. This visionary leadership not only guides the company through its evolutionary journey but also inspires and motivates the team, fostering a culture of ambition and forward-thinking that is essential for long-term success.

8. **Prioritize Hiring Top Talent:** Investing in high-caliber employees is non-negotiable. We've all heard stories of companies that attempted to cut costs by outsourcing overseas, only to find themselves micromanaging a team of less efficient contractors, ultimately resulting in frustration and diminished traction.

The key lies in building a lean, highly skilled team capable of delivering exceptional results efficiently. This approach streamlines operations, enhances service quality, fosters innovation, and drives sustained growth.

By concentrating on hiring "A" players, you ensure that your team is built with individuals who are not only experts in their fields but also deeply aligned with your company's vision and culture. This strategic focus on quality over quantity in staffing will set your brand apart, contributing to its success and distinguishing it from competitors.

In summary, while topics like email marketing and conversion optimization are crucial to a brand's success, it's these eight foundational strategies—focusing on key numbers that suggest value to potential buyers, vision, customer feedback, leadership, and hiring practices—that truly differentiate rich brands from the rest. These areas lay the groundwork for a brand not only to thrive in the present but also to be poised to generate future financial prosperity through its sale. In one case, a brand that was hoping to sell for $2 million got bought for $5 million.

Rich Brands That Fund the Owner and Their Investments

But what if you don't want to sell? That's perfectly fine as well. Some owners thrive on the idea of running a business they love, one that offers substantial owner distributions and a lifestyle that makes them feel alive. However, if long-term financial freedom is your goal, integrating strategic financial mechanisms, namely, pumps, buckets, and moats, into your operation can be transformative.

Pumps: The first step involves viewing your store as more than just a business; it's a revenue-generating machine that provides a steady stream of investable cash. This "pump" action is crucial. It's about optimizing your operations to maximize profitability, ensuring a consistent flow of cash that can be pulled out of the business and directed towards investments. Success here means having a well-oiled machine that, beyond covering operational costs and the owner's lifestyle expenses, generates surplus funds earmarked for further financial endeavors.

Buckets: Once you've established a reliable pump, the next move is to allocate a portion of these profits into "buckets"—investment vehicles that lean towards higher risks but also offer higher rewards, such as an aggressive stock portfolio. Unlike the volatile nature of store profits, which can plummet when your ad account takes a hit or fluctuates due to market trends and seasonality, wisely chosen buckets have the potential to exponentially grow your wealth through compounding over time. While revenue will always experience fluctuations—and your investments may to some extent as well—the power of compounding growth over time is truly mind-boggling. This step is about boldly reinvesting your gains in areas where they can work harder and smarter, thereby multiplying your financial base.

Moats: The concept of "moats" involves taking another portion of your financial gains, those generated from both pumps and successful buckets according to a pre-set rule, and investing them in lower-risk, stable vehicles. These investments are your safeguard, the protective barrier around your financial freedom castle. They might include bonds, dividend-yielding stocks, or even certain types of real estate that offer steady, predictable returns. While the excitement factor might be lower, the stability they provide is invaluable. Moats ensure that, regardless of how the market sways or what challenges your business faces, there's a solid foundation of financial wealth that remains untouched, offering security and peace of mind.

By effectively managing these three financial strategies, pumps, buckets, and moats, you not only maintain the joy and fulfillment of running a business you love but also lay down the tracks for substantial, sustainable financial freedom. This approach allows you to enjoy the best of both worlds: the entrepreneurial thrill of growing a brand you're passionate about and the strategic accumulation of wealth that secures your long-term financial well-being. The best part is that even if you just maintain revenue with this system in place, you will be funding investments that are compounding and increasing over time.

Most people think entrepreneurs play the game of business because they are fueled by greed and only care about money, but often, it's actually the opposite. Entrepreneurs want to solve their money problems so they never have to worry about them again.

Who is more obsessed with money, the person who bases every purchasing decision on affordability, often opting for the cheapest option without realizing they are choosing the lowest-quality version of life, or the person who doesn't think twice before seizing an opportunity to bless their spouse or deciding to get a check-up at the doctor without worrying about the cost?

Growing up, my family didn't have much money. I hated getting hurt, not because it hurt but because it would inevitably lead to stressful arguments about whether we should go to the doctor, making me feel like a burden to my parents. I felt guilty. I saw them kick serious and scary health issues down the road because we couldn't afford the care. Similarly, I felt guilty for wanting to do things that cost money, like playing football or joining the wrestling club.

I share this because, for whatever reason, the world doesn't always welcome change, and often, as your financial strength grows, you may face resistance. It could be an offhand joke from your parents, a hesitation to fully chase your dreams, guilt about the freedom and purchases your financial situation allows, or even the need to find new friends because some of your old ones are set on being broke and don't want to see you succeed. Whatever the case, I want you to realize that money is neither inherently good nor bad. It's just a tool, and it's perfectly okay to want more of it and enjoy the game where more money is your reward.

I don't think anyone truly believes money is evil, but we often hear sayings like "The root of all evil is the love of money." This phrase, originating from the Bible (1 Timothy 6:10), does not condemn money itself. Instead, Paul, the author, warns against letting money dominate one's life and values. Money, inherently neutral, is simply a tool, a means to facilitate exchange, achieve dreams, secure comfort, and extend generosity.

Key Takeaways:

- **Two Types of Poor Brands:** The two types are those that are overly reliant on ads and those that achieve organic growth but fail to implement ads effectively for further growth.

- **Over-Reliance on Ads:** Brands may become too dependent on advertising for growth, which can make them vulnerable when ad performance declines.

- **Organic Growth Limitations:** Brands that succeed organically but don't harness ads effectively miss opportunities to scale and reach new heights.

- **Rich Brand Characteristics:** These characteristics include building a strong brand identity, maintaining a solid AOV to LTV ratio, effective customer acquisition, lean operations, building cash reserves, basing decisions on customer feedback, visionary leadership, and prioritizing top talent hiring.

- **Financial Freedom Strategies:** These strategies emphasize the importance of financial management through "pumps" (revenue-generating mechanisms), "buckets" (high-risk, high-reward investments), and "moats" (low-risk, stable investments) for sustainable wealth creation.

- **Money as a Tool:** Money is a neutral tool that, when used wisely, can facilitate achieving dreams, ensuring comfort, and practicing generosity.

CHAPTER 5

Unlocking the Sales Frenzy: How to Build a Brand and Create Content That Converts Like Crazy

I once facetiously made the argument that if ads aren't working, it's because the brand sucks. It was a blunt statement but a slightly true one.

This left a lot of good people in the ecommerce world slightly offended and wondering, *Well, if my brand truly isn't up to par, what can I do to fix it? How can I be like the brands that seem to have the golden touch? You know, the ones that day after day, week after week, and year after year publish content that puts their competitors to shame and that don't just create tidal waves of sales but movements that people can't get enough of?*

To answer those questions, we first need to understand the differences between just running ads, which can be better described as direct-response marketing strategies, and brand building.

Without a solid branding and positioning strategy, your brand will be weak, and your ads will never work. This seems obvious, but our experience with and observation of thousands of stores suggests that it is not. Branding and positioning are the engines, and ads are the tires. Most brands will waste surprising amounts of time and money changing their tires over and over in hopes of getting movement while failing to see that they have a broken engine.

To the untrained eye, it's all just marketing, right? If it's not working, isn't it a good idea to keep trying different things? Not exactly. That's what amateurs do, not brands on the road to eight figures and beyond.

Let's start with brand, or more accurately, branding and positioning, one of the most widely debated ideas in marketing. Google "branding," and you will see an endless amount of definitions and frameworks.

What do you think of when you hear the word "branding"? Is it the logo, fonts, colors, and imagery that a company uses to create an identity for itself and differentiate itself from competitors selling similar products? Is saying that you have a "brand" just an easier way to say that you have a product-based, direct-to-consumer company? Is it the act of marking livestock with fire-heated marks to identify ownership? Or is it something entirely different?

Branding and positioning are a little bit of all those things and more… Well, in this case, branding and positioning may not involve literally burning symbols and letters into cows, but they certainly include the process of creating a distinct identity in the minds of your target audience and the market at large. Branding consists of a company's name and logo, visual identity design, mission, values, and tone of voice. Your brand is also determined by the quality and uniqueness of your products, the customer service experience you provide, and even your pricing strategy.

But finally, and arguably most importantly, your brand is your reputation, according to the words of others. It's what other people are saying about you regardless of what you say about yourself. You can be as aspirational as you want, but if you say you're known for the best burger in town while all your reviews say otherwise, then your brand isn't really known for having the best burger in town. You can say whatever mission statement you want, but if you say your brand is committed to putting out high-quality products and user experience but people don't actually agree with you, those are just empty words that nobody cares about. What really matters is what your customers say and what they vote on with their dollars.

On the other hand, direct-response marketing is a type of marketing strategy where the goal is to encourage an immediate response from consumers to quickly generate new leads or make a sale. A lot of people in ecommerce have relied on this method exclusively for building their stores and creating momentum. This is all good and dandy until results tank and you're left kicking and clawing to keep your businesses alive.

Relationship Equity

The only way to determine how much effort to put towards brand building versus direct response marketing is to view both of these activities through the lens of relationship equity.

In ecommerce, we don't have personal relationships with most of our customers. Instead, we use techniques to nurture relationships at scale by using the concept of relationship equity. Relationship equity is the affinity we build with our prospective clients prior to them giving us money. Marketing is a delicate balancing act between building and withdrawing relationship equity from your customers in exchange for sales.

The action of branding builds relationship equity, whereas running direct-response marketing, ads that ask your customers to buy, withdraws relationship equity. With this understanding, you can clearly see that if you are unable to consistently build and replenish relationship equity with your audience, your ads will fatigue, and your customers will begin to despise you. They will view you as a needy person who is always asking and never giving. Nobody likes that person, and nobody wants to be that person, yet brands unintentionally act like that person all the time and then wonder why they can't get results.

Direct-response marketing is hyper-focused on calculating return on investment (ROI) in shorter time frames. For example, "What was the ROAS of our Facebook ads last week?" This type of marketing isn't concerned with the big picture, whereas branding only sees the bigger picture and operates off of longer-term time preferences. Branding is holistic in nature, and though it takes much longer to build, it goes much further and compounds quicker over time.

Ads alone often generate quick wins, but many stores burn out because they lose all their relationship equity in the process. When this happens, people become indifferent. They stop engaging, clicking, and buying. Their sentiment has changed, and the affinity is gone.

Companies that focus on branding alone will also go broke if they never figure out how to ask for the order and draw on some of that equity. And companies that focus only on direct-response marketing and running ads will go broke because everyone hates them for trying to sell all the time. Nobody likes someone who takes, takes, and takes but never gives. So, there's a balance, right?

Let me be clear: there's absolutely nothing wrong with running ads and asking for the order. In fact, your ability to do so is vital to your longevity and growth as long as you understand if and when you have equity available to withdraw.

To sell products successfully, you need both. The best marketing strategies build relationship equity while simultaneously inviting people to transact. A strong brand hedges the volatility of ads and lays a foundation for its success, and powerful direct-response marketing, when done correctly, creates explosive growth and amplifies a solid brand.

A strong brand can shut down ads for a month and be okay. It can experience spikes and dips in its direct-response marketing and still grow. Most of the smaller brands out there don't have this figured out, but that's okay because a lot can be done to strengthen them.

Most people are pretty good at running ads but fall short when it comes to actually creating the inner workings of a brand that scales to eight figures and beyond. In the remainder of this chapter, we will examine the science of what actually works (and what doesn't). We will transition from having a vague idea about concepts like "being likable" and "adding value" to having clear levers to pull and actions to take. The following information will empower you to build a brand and create content that sells like crazy, making your ads seem like they magically work, scale with ease, and never fatigue.

Five Keys to Building a Brand and Creating Content That Sells Like Crazy

1. Building Relationship Equity

Research shows that up to 95% of decisions are made based on emotions, which demonstrates that how your customers feel about you is actually more important than what they think about you. But how do we effectively influence the way someone feels about our brand, and how do we create content that actually builds relationship equity at scale?

We've all heard phrases like "Value first!" "Give your audience value!" and "Value, value, value!" But what does that actually mean? And if doing this is truly a cornerstone of building a brand and generating orders, how does one actually devise a plan for "providing value"? Let's make it easy.

Marketers have used four powerful methods for decades to build relationship equity with their audiences. To instantly become the apple of your audience's eye, you simply need to choose one or two and apply them consistently.

No matter which method you choose, remember that understanding your audience is the foundation for successfully building relationship equity. You must deeply know your audience—what resonates with them, their preferences, challenges, hopes, and dreams, and even what they find humorous. This understanding is vital across all methods to ensure your efforts in building relationship equity are well-received and effective.

Make Your Audience Laugh: The first method for building relationship equity is through humor. If you can make your audience laugh and bring joy into their world, you will deposit equity into the relationship and make your brand more relatable and approachable. To get you thinking in the right direction, here are some easy ways to incorporate humor effectively into your marketing and strengthen connections with your audience.

Make light of the common problems or pain points that your product or service aims to solve. This not only shows that you deeply understand their challenges but also humanizes your brand.

For instance, if you sell big-and-tall t-shirts, creating memes that humorously address the struggles of finding well-fitting clothes can be a hit. Phrases like "Thanks for the shirt" on a visibly tight shirt showing a fuzzy navel or "Yes, I love it… Thanks, Mom" can make your audience chuckle, see their own experiences reflected, and feel bonded to your brand.

While humor can be a powerful tool, it's important to balance it with informative and valuable brand content that creates a desire for the product. Your audience should come to see you as entertaining, helpful, and most definitely someone they want to buy from, not just another meme page. When you post about your products, you want people to feel excited and not caught off guard. If they are only there for the laughs and want nothing to do with your business, you know you've taken the humor too far. Consistency in your humor is key to keeping your audience engaged, but it should not overshadow the products and value your brand provides.

Pay close attention to how your audience responds to your humorous content. What works for one brand or audience might not work for another. If certain types of humor receive a positive response while others fall flat, use this feedback to refine your approach. Engaging with your audience's reactions, whether through comments, shares, or likes, can provide valuable insights into their preferences and make them feel like they are a valuable part of your community.

Brands that excel in this area do not limit their humorous content to just one platform. They integrate it into their email marketing, website copy, and even customer service interactions where appropriate. This approach creates a cohesive brand personality that is consistently engaging and personable across all touchpoints.

Finally, make sure that what you put out aligns with your overall brand voice and values. The humor should feel like a natural extension of your brand, not a forced or misaligned attempt to be funny. When you effectively use humor in your marketing strategy, you make your brand more relatable, approachable, and memorable. It's about striking the right balance between making your audience laugh and providing them with tasteful invitations to purchase.

Remember, the goal is to deposit boatloads of relationship equity into your relationship with your audience, so much so that buying your products becomes almost a way for them to say thank you.

Need a great example? Check out Chubbie's Instagram page.

Make Your Audience Feel Something: In 2020, on a bright, snowy day, my multi-generational family and I were snugly huddled around the TV, watching the Super Bowl. The house buzzed with vibrant energy, laughter, and the aroma of scrumptious food. Yet, as a commercial began, a sudden hush fell over the room, pierced only by the serene, slightly melancholy notes of a piano. We watched as words slowly appeared in Google's search bar: "How… to… not… forget."

An elderly man's voice, tender and full of longing, said, "Hey, Google, show me pictures of Loretta." What followed was a poignant slideshow revealing the rich tapestry of a life shared between him and his wife, Loretta, accompanied by his heartfelt pleas to remember. He instructed Google, "Remember that Loretta hated my mustache," "Remember Loretta loved going to Alaska and eating scallops," and so forth. In this way, he guided us through a series of cherished memories—anniversary celebrations, youthful escapades—all paired with the heavy weight of a looming goodbye, the anguish of a man grappling with the erosion of his most precious memories.

With a final, emotional declaration, "Remember I am the luckiest man in the world," set against a backdrop of the requests being cataloged for reminiscence, the commercial gently segued into on-screen text, "*A little help with the little things.*" As the screen faded to white, the scene concluded with Google's logo. In about a minute, the excitement and bustle of a Super Bowl party had turned into a heartfelt reflection on the ones we love and the finality of life as a few people threw teary-eyed glances at our widowed grandma.

By adding sentiment to your marketing materials, you create a powerful emotional connection between your audience and your brand. When executed effectively, this approach can lead to surprisingly strong attachments to your brand, based more on emotional associations than what you actually do or sell. As a result, your audience becomes more engaged.

If you think this approach aligns with your brand but aren't sure where to start, consider the following ideas and how they might apply to you: give honor where it's due, acknowledge and show compassion for others' pain, express gratitude, especially for things that have come at a great cost, and create moments of remembrance and nostalgia.

Of the four methods, this can be the most powerful. Use it carefully, however, because if done poorly, it can backfire, creating equally strong but negative reactions. If people feel that you're manipulating their emotions to take their money, they will likely resent your brand.

For a couple of great examples of this method being used well, search for "Google | Loretta | Super Bowl [2020]" and "LEGO® Advert: Let's Build."

Make Your Audience Feel Like They Are a Part of Something: Humans have a deep need for belonging. I believe we were beautifully designed with a need for community, and by facilitating community, we can help people become happier. My challenge to you is not to view this information merely as an opportunity to enhance your marketing but to live it out in a way that genuinely improves people's lives. If you can do this, you will build more momentum than you know what to do with and make the world a better place as a result.

Among many others, organizations like Harley-Davidson and Patagonia have excelled not just in making their audience feel like they're part of something bigger but also in genuinely enhancing their customers' lives. Harley-Davidson has built a global community of enthusiasts and riders who share a deep passion for the brand. Through events, clubs, and online forums, Harley-Davidson fosters a sense of belonging among its customers, making them feel like part of an exclusive group.

Patagonia has successfully created a community around environmental activism and outdoor sports. They engage their customers through initiatives like the "Worn Wear" program, environmental documentaries, and advocacy for environmental causes, making their customers feel they are part of a movement to save the planet.

For a few more great examples of this method in action, search for "APPLE | Think Different" and "Dodge 'Farmer' Super Bowl Ad."

Give Value to Your Audience: Finally, giving away free value is the fourth surefire way to build relationship equity with your audience and establish yourself as an authority. This strategy works exceptionally well in markets where consumers are aware of solutions. A prime example would be a supplement company that runs an educational blog on healthy living. Another would be a clothing brand, like Cuts Clothing, offering free style guides or helping people select the right clothing for their body type.

Looking for an example of a brand that adopts a value-first approach to building relationship equity? Check out the blog section of Boom! by Cindy Joseph.

Boom! prides itself on being the world's first pro-age cosmetic and skincare line. They provide all sorts of useful information for aging women on how to embrace their age rather than fight it. In doing so, they build trust and affinity and generate tens of millions of dollars in annual revenue.

2. Provide a Specific Solution to a Specific Person

There's a phrase we used to say around the office: "The riches are in the niches." You can't be everything to everybody, so it's much better to narrow your focus to the person you are best suited to serve and then serve them better than anyone else can. I am often blown away by the sheer number of products that were created—and eventually grew into multi-million dollar brands—by someone simply trying to solve a very specific problem they were struggling with, only to find out that millions of other people had the exact same issue.

Focusing on providing a specific solution to a specific person isn't simply a strategic choice; it's a pathway to unlocking more money in your market. When you narrow your target and tailor your offering, your marketing and sales efforts become exponentially more efficient. You're able to communicate directly and effectively with your audience, resonating with them on a deeper level and converting shoppers into buyers. This precision in targeting ensures that every marketing dollar spent works harder, yielding a better return on investment.

Catering to a specific niche makes your customers feel understood and gives them the impression that your service was custom-built to serve them, leading to enhanced customer loyalty and brand advocacy. Satisfied customers become vocal supporters of your brand, extending your reach organically and amplifying your marketing efforts without additional cost. This not only builds a strong, loyal customer base but also positions your brand as the preferred choice in your niche.

Be mindful of this brand-building key, but try not to overthink it. For many people, the specific solution could be as simple as providing a certain type of clothing to a specific demographic and then consistently delivering on that promise.

Below is the super-simple template for creating brand positioning statements that we often use with our clients to provide clarity on whom we're targeting and what value those people should expect to receive.

Brand Positioning Statement:

To [Target Market], [Your Brand] is the [Market Category] that delivers [Differentiators] so that [Solution to Customer Problems], because [Core Attributes].

First Example: To health-conscious individuals looking for natural and organic food options, GreenEats is the grocery store that delivers an extensive range of organic produce, sustainable goods, and wellness products so that customers can lead a healthier, eco-friendly lifestyle because we commit to quality, sustainability, and community wellness.

Second Example: To urban professionals in their 30s seeking a blend of style and sustainability, Eco Chic is the fashion brand that delivers ethically sourced and environmentally friendly apparel so that customers can express their personal style without compromising their values because we believe in transparency, quality, and the power of sustainable fashion to make a positive impact on the world.

Obviously, you wouldn't use these brand positioning statements as advertising or website copy, but you'd be surprised at how easy it is to write powerful copy once you've done a little work establishing your brand positioning statement.

When your solution addresses the unique needs of a specific audience, you can also command higher price points due to the perceived value of your offering. Customers are willing to invest more in products or services that seem tailor-made for them, especially when these solutions effectively address their specific challenges. It's the difference between a brain surgeon and a general practitioner.

One thing that I've seen over and over again is that people often worry about becoming too specific and missing out on sales, but targeting a specific audience also means you'll face lower competition. While others dilute their efforts by trying to appeal to the masses, you'll occupy a unique space in the market. This exclusivity not only makes it easier for customers to choose your brand over more generic options, but it also allows you to dominate your niche and enjoy a larger market share.

Finally, focusing on a specific solution for a specific person grants your business greater agility and the ability to innovate. You can quickly adapt to customer feedback and market changes, continually refining your offering to better meet the needs of your specific target audience because you can stop solving for the crowd and start solving for the individual. This constant evolution not only keeps you ahead of competitors but also increases the value you provide, encouraging ongoing customer engagement and repeat business.

Zeroing in on a specific solution for a specific group isn't just about making more money; it's about building a sustainable, profitable business that thrives by delivering significant value where it's most needed and appreciated.

3. Be Consistent

Building a strong brand and creating content that converts like crazy isn't just about being flashy or innovative; it's about being consistent and reliable in the sea of consumer choices. Consistency is maturity. It is a linchpin of brand strength and content conversion.

Consider the titans of industry and what they're known for. Rolex doesn't just sell watches; they sell unrivaled craftsmanship and timeless luxury. McDonald's isn't necessarily the best food available; it's the home of the Big Mac, where speed and taste meet affordability. Starbucks doesn't just sell coffee; they sell the same cup of coffee whether you're in Seattle or Miami. Costco and Walmart, each in their domain, promise and deliver value and convenience that customers depend on.

None of this is accidental. These brands have honed their identities around consistency, ensuring that every touchpoint with customers—be it product quality, customer service, or the in-store experience—reinforces what they stand for. We can do the same thing in the direct-to-consumer world online. This reliability builds trust, and trust is the currency of conversion. When customers know exactly what to expect, and those expectations are met, they don't just come back; they become evangelists. Notice that I didn't say "when those expectations are met or exceeded." Consistency is actually more powerful than exceeding expectations.

Now, take a moment to explore websites like Filson.com or Lululemon.com. These brands have crafted their narratives with such clarity that you cannot help but understand what they stand for at a glance. Filson promises rugged durability and timeless style for the outdoor enthusiast. Lululemon champions an active, high-quality lifestyle. Their consistency in messaging, aesthetics, and product quality sets a clear expectation: what you see is what you get, and what you get is exceptional.

So, what does your brand stand for? Does every piece of content you produce, every product you launch, and every customer interaction you have reinforce that identity? Or is there clutter—misaligned products, off-message content, confusing customer experiences—that dilutes your essence? Pruning away the non-essential, the off-brand, and the confusing allows your true identity to shine through with consistency.

Consistency is what makes a customer choose your coffee over another, your watch over the next, or your store for their individual needs. In a world where choices are endless, being the reliable choice for something specific is a powerful method of not just existing but excelling.

4. Distinguish Yourself From Your Competitors

Sometimes, when people identify what they stand for or what they want to be known for, they discover they are not the only ones taking that angle. This realization can be discouraging. However, if you talk to any professional musician, they will tell you it's all the same: everyone is using the same seven chords. Yet music holds the power to shape culture. It's the artist's personal flavor, emotions, and story that make the music unique. I would argue that the same approach can be very valuable when it comes to distinguishing yourself from your competitors. Maybe you aren't the OG of your space, but there is and only ever will be one *you*.

Are there any parts of your personal story that can be used to make your brand stand out? What unique angle can you take that your competitors aren't? What comparison can you draw between yourself and competing brands?

One iconic example of a campaign that helped a company distinguish itself from a more dominant competitor and subsequently increase its market share and revenue is Apple's "Get a Mac" campaign. From 2006 to 2009, Apple ran a campaign designed to compare its Macintosh computers favorably against

PCs, which predominantly ran Microsoft's Windows operating system, a much larger competitor in terms of market share.

The "Get a Mac" campaign was a series of TV commercials and ads that featured two characters: "Mac," portrayed as a young, casual, and cool guy, and "PC," portrayed as a stuffy, awkward, and somewhat outdated businessman. Each commercial showcased conversations between Mac and PC, humorously highlighting the perceived advantages of Mac computers, such as ease of use, lack of viruses, better entertainment and creative software, and fewer technical issues. All of these feature differences were clearly communicated in the advertisements, but something deeper and more powerful was happening beneath the surface. Apple was planting the idea that cool people use Macs and boring nerds use PCs—an idea that is still very much alive today.

This campaign was highly successful for several reasons:

- **Clear Differentiation:** It clearly distinguished Macs from PCs in a fun and memorable way, making it easy for consumers to understand the benefits of a Mac over a PC.

- **Emotional Appeal:** By personifying the computers, Apple was able to create an emotional connection with its audience. The cool and relaxed demeanor of Mac contrasted with the uptight and frequently troubled PC, making Macs more appealing to a younger, creative demographic.

- **Brand Reinforcement:** The campaign reinforced Apple's brand image as innovative, user-friendly, and the choice for creative individuals. This helped attract customers who valued these qualities.

- **Viral Effect:** The humorous and engaging ads were widely shared, extending their reach beyond traditional advertising mediums.

The effectiveness of the "Get a Mac" campaign was reflected in Apple's increased market share and sales of Macintosh computers during and after the campaign. It helped Apple solidify its position as a serious competitor in the personal computer market despite Microsoft's dominance. This campaign is often cited in marketing textbooks and courses as an exemplary case of brand differentiation.

I also want to point out that "distinguishing yourself from your competitors is important even if you don't feel that your products are superior. The idea that one brand sits at the top of the food chain and all others are junky and less valuable is nonsense. Every product or service brings something unique to the table, appealing to specific needs and tastes. It's all about identifying these unique selling points and showcasing them to the right audience. Every product has its own set of strengths and weaknesses, and the key is to understand these aspects and tailor your marketing strategy accordingly.

Consider your customers' needs. Not everyone is looking for the most advanced features or the highest quality. For instance, someone who only needs a sewing machine for the occasional repair job doesn't need the latest, most sophisticated model designed for serious enthusiasts.

Budget is another crucial factor. Not all customers are willing or able to splurge on the most expensive option. For some, affordability is the most important thing, and they might prefer a more cost-effective solution that meets their basic needs without breaking the bank.

What might be considered an "inferior" product can actually be the smarter choice for consumers based on their specific requirements, preferences, and financial constraints.

Distinguishing yourself isn't about reinventing the wheel but about adding your unique flavor to it. It's about understanding that in a world where many may sell similar products or services, your personal touch and the unique perspective you bring can make all the difference.

5. Have a Clear Value Proposition

At the end of the day, founders must position their brands to address one crucial question from customers: "Why should I choose to buy from you?" Contrary to popular belief, doing this effectively does not merely involve offering discount codes or providing free shipping on orders over $50. What we're really talking about is the combination of a solid pricing strategy or product offer with a unique value proposition that instantly communicates the essence of how this product will improve your customers' lives. It's a clear revelation of the value your customer will receive upon making a purchase.

In 2001, the race to bring the best MP3 player technology to the market was well underway. Companies were innovating and bursting with excitement over the revolutionary idea of transitioning from bulky cassette and CD players to digital music on an MP3 player.

What Steve Jobs recognized and that everyone else didn't was that the overall value proposition was just as important as (and maybe even more important than) the quality of the product. While everyone else was trying to sell this bitrate or that amount of storage at these discount prices and using technical terms that no one really understood or cared about, Steve Jobs offered people the opportunity to have "1,000 songs in their pocket." It was simple. It was concise. It was powerful.

Like other Apple products, many could argue that the iPod was not the most technically superior or capable MP3 player on the market. However, for the next two and a half years, no contender threatened to dethrone the iPod. By early 2004, Apple had secured 92% of the digital audio player market.

In the following nine years, Steve Jobs guided Apple in launching several more products that dominated the market, efforts that ultimately made it America's first trillion-dollar company.

That is the power of having a clear offer.

Crafting Your Value Proposition

Every concept discussed in this chapter converges at this pivotal moment, laying the groundwork for crafting a compelling value proposition. Understanding how to build equity with your audience, offering a specific solution to a specific person, establishing trust through consistency, and distinguishing yourself from the competition are all critical steps. But now, these elements must be woven together seamlessly to form a singular, impactful message: your value proposition—your unique version of "1,000 songs in your pocket."

Your value proposition will likely consist of one to two sentences that clearly describe the benefit your customers will receive. It should be unique to you and strategically positioned against your competitors. Your value proposition creates opportunities for you to build equity with your customers. It can be repackaged in several different ways based on short-term goals, paired with a unique pricing strategy, and, most importantly, it fuels the success of all your sales and marketing endeavors.

Here are some real-life phrases that encapsulate the essence of these brands' value propositions:

- **Cuts Clothing:** "Workleisure for the modern professional."

- **Badlands Gear:** "We're unconditional. Unmistakable. We're Badlands, and we make the best hunting apparel, packs, and accessories on the planet."

- **Ten Thousand:** "The only training shorts you'll ever need."

- **Airbnb:** "Belong anywhere."

- **Disney:** "The happiest place on Earth."

- **Old Spice:** "The original. If your grandfather hadn't worn it, you wouldn't exist."

- **BMW:** "The ultimate driving machine." "Sheer driving pleasure."

- **Levi's:** "Quality never goes out of style."

- **Amazon**: "And you're done."

- **Lululemon:** "Fashionable and functional."

- **Gucci:** "Exquisite Italian craftsmanship, providing customers with high-quality products and great attention to the design of its products."

So, the next time you're scratching your head, pulling your hair out, or cursing at your computer because your ads don't seem to be working, consider asking yourself the following questions:

- Am I actively building relationship equity with my customers or just asking everyone to buy?

- Am I providing a specific solution for a specific person?

- Am I showing my audience consistency in what I want my brand to be known for?

- Am I actively distinguishing myself from my competitors?

- Is my value proposition clear? In other words, are the benefits that my customers will receive once they buy clearly and persuasively communicated to them?

If your answer to any of these questions is "no" or even "not really," stop working on your ads and start building your brand because your direct-response marketing efforts will eventually burn out if they haven't already.

Key Takeaways:

- **Building Relationship Equity:** Engage your audience with humor, emotions, community, and value to build strong, positive associations with your brand. This involves creating content that resonates on a personal level, fostering a sense of connection and loyalty.

- **Provide Specific Solutions to Specific People:** Focus on serving a well-defined target audience with tailored solutions. This will enhance the efficiency of your marketing efforts and improve customer loyalty. This niche focus allows for clearer messaging and higher conversion rates.

- **Consistency Is Key:** Maintain a consistent brand message, look, and customer experience across all platforms and interactions. This reliability builds trust, which is crucial for conversions and customer retention.

- **Distinguish Yourself From Competitors:** Use unique aspects of your personal story or brand philosophy to stand out in a crowded market. Highlighting what makes your brand different encourages customers to choose you over competitors.

- **Clear Value Proposition:** Develop a compelling value proposition that succinctly communicates the value your product or service brings to customers. This clarity helps make your brand's benefits immediately apparent, facilitating quicker purchasing decisions.

CHAPTER 6

The Secret to Bulletproofing Your Sales

As much as we'd like for it not to be the case, sales rarely tank for just one reason. Similarly, they can't be fixed with a single simple action. Sales usually decline due to a combination of many small issues accumulating to create one large, unfavorable outcome.

Marketing is a complex system and must be addressed as such. However, we should find encouragement in the words of Dr. W. Edwards Deming: "Every system is perfectly designed to get the result that it does." This suggests that we have the power to redesign our marketing for a better and more favorable outcome. Deming estimates that 94% of problems in a business are caused by systems that are not functioning as needed rather than by individual actions.

Okay, so what's the point? The point is, if you've ever felt like you traded your nine-to-five for a 24/7, there's a way to change all of that. If you find yourself constantly struggling to keep your sales afloat, as if you're in a leaky boat frantically bailing out water just to stay ahead, there's a way to change all of that. If you are frustrated because the whole idea was to live life on your own terms, but now you're just watching all your money go down the drain, there's a way to change all of that. If you are pissed off or even nauseous by the fact that sales were popping off this time last year, but now you don't even want to eat breakfast anymore because you can't seem to hit the same numbers or find the sales consistency you're after, there's a way to change all of that.

With a clear understanding of the components that create a successful marketing system, it's actually not very difficult.

Learning how to create sales consistency was a lesson Daniel and I had to learn the hard way. Remember back in Chapter 2 when I promised I'd share the story of our great fall? Well, buckle up because it's time. I share this story not because I need or even really want you to know it but because I believe our trials and tribulations, our walk through the valley of the shadow of death, will give you clear options on your journey towards revenue growth, consistency, and personal freedom. These are things I genuinely wish for you, and the idea that I can help people achieve them gets me out of bed every day and puts the wind in my sails.

My Story

To tell this story in the most effective and accurate way possible, I want to first give you a little bit of context, including the fact that my Christian faith (and Daniel's) deeply influences the way we navigate situations like this, before bringing you into the juicy details of our downfall. Consider yourself privileged. This is not information I share with most.

I was born into a family on its way out of dysfunction. My dad is a recovering alcoholic and had a long history of numbing pain with drugs. In my younger years, though there was a lot of healing and progress in our home, there were still certain dysfunctional dynamics that would appear, including the classic situation where, out of our brokenness, we all co-dependently fell into certain roles to keep the peace.

Early on, I felt like I took on the role of the golden boy in our family. I thought that I could control the chaos around me by being "good." This belief drove me to become a high performer who never asked for anything so as not to be a burden to the people who had real needs, like my dad or my siblings who were in crisis. I always smiled, and when I kept my room nice and tidy, I felt safe. I thought the better I was, the less pain I and my family would feel. Sadly, I felt that I had the ability to earn love.

That was how I viewed the world. This view followed me throughout my life and seemingly served me well through a lot of situations. As a young boy, I was very well-liked and voted the most handsome boy in Mrs. Mee's sixth-grade class. I won state wrestling championships, helped lead football teams to win state titles, personally broke school records, and won accolades not just in wrestling and football but also in track and field. When they tallied up votes for who would be the next class president, I was told by the staff that they had never seen such a landslide victory as when I was elected. I was genuinely a kind and gifted boy who loved life and others with no real agenda and minimal insecurities.

More recently, my golden boy role approach to life empowered me to successfully do the commercial fishing thing for a number of years and then eventually pivot and grow Shopanova, our ecommerce growth agency, from the ground up with Dan. We successfully built the life of our dreams, complete with large salaries, freedom over our schedules, and work that we love with an awesome team. And since we had a million dollars safely stashed away in the bank, we were going to begin splitting and distributing the $150 thousand in profit coming into our business each month moving forward.

The Downturn

Life as a golden boy is great when everything is going well, but what happens when everything starts to crumble?

Five years into scaling our company and getting amazing results for our clients, iOS 14 hit. If you're not familiar with what this is, the short explanation is that iOS 14 was an update Apple made that changed the default settings of an iPhone to basically make online behavior invisible to advertisers unless the user explicitly opts in to being tracked. Though we had been preparing for this for over a year, the change hit us like a hurricane, affecting not only our ability to run effective advertising and get clients for our company but for every single client that we served.

Performance began to dip, and we slowly began to lose clients. To stop the bleeding, we went all in on finding solutions for our clients and put our own marketing on the back burner. At the time, we were spending over $125,000 a month on Facebook ads. Everybody in business knows that nothing ever moves in a straight line, and this is especially true for businesses with longer sales cycles, so, for the most part, we held course.

It was very common for us to spend a lot of money to create a large pipeline of potential clients that would then convert the following month. You have to spend money to make money, and our ability to stomach this grew incrementally as we increased ad spend over the years from $1,500 a month to well over a hundred grand per month.

With the busy season just around the corner and a need to replace clients, we felt like the best choice was to keep spending. Initially, we spent the same amount but got a little less back in return, so we dropped ad spend the following month to recalibrate.

Again, we got just a little bit less back than what we were used to. This cycle repeated itself until, eventually, our credit cards were maxed out, and we had no pipeline of new customers.

About this same time, a member of our leadership team decided that it was time for him to venture off and start his own agency. This would leave a dent in what we did, and we would miss him, but we were confident we could find someone to fill his shoes and keep moving forward, no big deal. Shortly after he left, we began seeing his name pop up in a couple of our biggest clients' Facebook business managers, and then, all of a sudden, we were removed. That was weird. Then, it happened again and again and again. Not only did he go behind our backs to recruit over a hundred thousand dollars worth of monthly recurring revenue in this situation, but he also recruited a few of our key players to go with him.

I felt blindsided and betrayed. I was furious because I felt as though I had given this young guy a great job opportunity and the ability to ascend inside a booming company with a great work culture. I actually take pride and find joy in going above and beyond for our team to provide them with a meaningful, lucrative, and joyful career, so this really hurt. I was also mad because my ability to employ the other people on the team, whom I also deeply cared about and believed in, was now taken away when our clients, whom we spent tens of thousands of dollars acquiring, chose to walk away for a lower price with the guy who'd left.

I kept telling myself that it would all be fine. This wasn't the first time I had faced hard things in my life. Dan and I continued showing up day after day, doing what we could and doing our best to surrender the rest to God and trust that it would all work out. We desperately needed a miracle because all of the evidence around us made it clear that we were on a direct path to bankruptcy. I couldn't sleep. I either had no appetite at all or an insatiable desire to devour junk food, and I began feeling anxious pretty much around the clock.

To find moments of peace, I would think about the good things in my life. I thought about my beautiful wife, the beautiful home I had been blessed enough to build her, and my four sun-kissed, bleach-blond kiddos and the fifth one on its way. I would distract myself at work by thinking about the greenhouse we'd built, how good the salsa made from homegrown vegetables was going to taste, the playhouse we were building, the hikes available to us in the great outdoors of Alaska, the midnight sun, the kids' baseball games, and all the summer adventures we'd go on.

For the first time since fishing and construction, I began to compartmentalize my life again and separate work from home. I even began to use my life at home as an escape from a job that I was growing weary of. Unfortunately, the stress of losing clients, having to fire close friends, and watching the business slowly burn to the ground was so heavy on me that it began coming out sideways at home.

The problem with believing that I could somehow perform or earn my way to a feeling of significance, security, and love was the fact that no matter how hard I tried, I was failing—and through the logic of my own broken belief, the fact that I was failing meant that I was not significant, safe, or loved anymore. I was a little boy in a man's body, smack dab in the middle of a full-blown crisis. I had a massive hole in my heart, and when God would not fix my problems, I began looking to my wife, Brittani, for comfort.

My refuge at home slowly turned into just another thing that I desperately needed to escape, which actually felt much worse and scarier than anything at work because my family is my life. My wife and children are literally at the top of my priorities and my reason for living. Long story short, Brittani and I began fighting a lot. I made several very poor decisions, and the feeling of not being safe or loved that I once knew as a kid in a dysfunctional home was stronger now than ever. I felt worthless and rejected. My wife felt inadequate and unloved. The next thing I knew, I was sitting in marriage counseling, fighting to keep my marriage alive, too.

With the summer basically ruined, I began coaching myself through the hard times by focusing ahead to Christmas, when I would hold our newborn baby for the first time. Having had four kids already, I knew that in those precious moments when a baby is taking its first breaths, the earth stands still, and nothing else matters but that moment. When we found out that Brittani had miscarried the baby, I fell into a deep depression.

A few days before Thanksgiving, Dan and I had to do another round of layoffs. In that group of people was a close friend of mine who was in the middle of trying to purchase a house and move his family back into the United States from a foreign country. I felt like a fraud, and laying off people who trusted me for their income filled me with shame.

Christmas was hard because I was grieving the loss of our baby, which felt extra hard because it brought up all the pain of the first miscarriage we'd had several years prior. I wanted to be excited, but I wasn't. Now, alongside the pain was more shame about not being able to be fully present and celebrate with my kids during one of our favorite times of the year.

A couple of months later, in February, Daniel, who was also barely keeping his head above water and doing his best to navigate new trauma while simultaneously fending off PTSD from rolling his boat, was called away from work to be with his wife, who has since been diagnosed with bipolar syndrome. She went through a terrible cycle of ups and downs and was bedridden for six months. This led to Daniel needing to be home for months, taking care of his wife and children while we continued to crash and burn as a business.

We lost more clients and had to fire more of our team, and every time we thought the business was back on track, something unexpected happened, and it fell apart again.

My son Oliver had been born with his skull plates fused together and, as a one-year-old, needed skull reconstruction surgery. Years later, during our downfall, I found myself driving Oliver four hours to Anchorage for a doctor's appointment about an upcoming eye surgery. We were uncertain if we could afford the procedure he now needed. On that long drive, I remember feeling like that was it. We were done. I was done.

Despite Alaska's majestic open scenery, I felt as if the world was closing in. I felt like a complete failure. The day was sunny and beautiful, but all I saw was darkness. *I can't fix this business,* I told myself. *I can't keep my marriage alive, I can't keep my kids alive, and I can't even take care of myself.* It became hard to breathe, and I began having chest pains.

There I was, fresh into my thirties, thinking that I was having a heart attack. I went to the doctor a few days later, and when I found out I had not suffered a heart attack, I realized I was disappointed. I realized that I wanted so badly to escape that I would prefer death or near death to facing my circumstances. I thought that if I were hospitalized with something serious, at least I would get the rest and refreshment my soul and body needed.

In an 18-month-long whirlwind of a dumpster fire, Dan and I drained all of our cash despite repeatedly cutting expenses beyond what was comfortable or even healthy for the business and taking massive personal pay cuts. We leveraged the office that we'd built for more working capital, and I pulled a line of credit on my home to raise enough money to meet payroll. We went from feeling like we couldn't lose to having a negative net worth to the tune of multiple six figures. As you can imagine, we were barely hanging on.

What My Story Means for You

I share these details with you, most of which not even close friends and family know, for two reasons.

First, the most valuable thing I can offer you, regardless of the setting or circumstances, is hope. Before I show you the business strategies we used to rewrite our story and how you can bulletproof your sales, avoid going through what we did, and create the breakthrough you're after, I must authentically and boldly acknowledge that the biggest ingredient for our success out of this situation was, and continues to be, the hope found in a relationship with a loving Father. Others may feel differently and have different beliefs, and that's totally fine, but I would be remiss and even lying if I didn't acknowledge the role this has played in our business.

At the end of the day, if we ask ourselves why we want sales enough times, we get to the basic human needs of purpose, understanding, belonging, security, significance, and love. I have consciously and unconsciously deployed many strategies to the point of utter exhaustion in an attempt to fix my problems and get those needs met, only to find that all my efforts fall short.

The most valuable gift I've received from my business journey, through both good times and bad, is a deeper and clearer understanding that God is the only reliable and perfect source for those needs. Understanding and leaning into that reality has truly set me free and allowed me to build a life and business that I truly love.

I also share this story because it illuminates a path forward that's rooted in real results, one Dan and I, and many others, have used and that we can now break down into actionable concepts. The Codex framework I am about to share with you was built by a business coach of mine named Taylor Welch, and I give him the credit. I have simply taken the concepts and adapted them from a service-based business model into one that is relevant to direct-to-consumer companies.

The Codex

The Codex serves not just as a guideline for healthy growth but also as a comprehensive strategy for building a business that allows the owner to thrive. It is built on three components: attention, demonstration, and monetization. Each plays a crucial role in attracting customers, showcasing products and brand value, and ultimately securing sales and fostering business growth.

When constructed correctly, the system not only provides flexibility, allowing ecommerce businesses to customize its application to their unique situation and goals, but also ensures durability. Had Dan and I built our business according to the principles of the Codex, we likely could have avoided 18 months of stress, decline, and near bankruptcy.

Components of the Codex

- **Attention** – This represents the marketing efforts to capture the potential customer's interest and can be divided into four categories:

    - **Paid Social:** Includes having a paid advertising strategy on platforms like Facebook, Instagram, TikTok, and Pinterest.

    - **Paid Search:** Comprises search engine marketing through Google Ads, YouTube Ads, and Microsoft Ads.

    - **Organic:** Entails non-paid strategies on social platforms, such as Facebook, Instagram, TikTok, and Pinterest.

    - **Outbound:** Covers methods like affiliates and influencers that proactively reach out to potential customers outside the company's platforms.

- **Demonstration** – After you have a solid asset in place for consistently generating attention, you must then nurture customers by showcasing the products and the brand value with a demonstration asset. There are four main ways we do this:

- **Website:** Typically, an ecommerce store built on Shopify or a platform like it.

- **Special Offer Pages:** Dedicated landing pages designed to highlight special deals or products.

- **Email and SMS:** Campaigns and automated flows that are often employed to transition people from merely having their attention captured to being effectively educated about the products, thus transforming them into legitimate shoppers.

- **On-Platform Shops:** Direct-sales channels within social media platforms like Facebook/Instagram Shops and TikTok Shops.

• **Monetization** – The final step focuses on generating revenue through various conversion assets. This includes:

- **Offers:** Special deals designed to encourage purchasing, either generally or in larger quantities, based on a set of incentives, such as first-order discounts, free shipping thresholds, product bundles, and upsells.

- **Individual Products:** Selling single items without any bundling or special offers.

- **Wholesale:** Selling products in bulk to retailers or other business entities.

- **Repeat Purchases:** When existing customers purchase again or get on some kind of subscription plan.

- **Brick and Mortar Retail:** The traditional retail model, selling products in physical stores.

Though breaking down the attention, demonstration, and monetization assets can provide clarity on what makes a business work, the magic is not in the components but in the phases of implementation based on where the business is.

Most brands that launch successfully do so by intuiting the approach described by Sean Frank, nine-figure CEO and founder of Ridge:

"If I was starting today, what I'd do is get very good at creating content and have products that people love and are visually appealing. This is all I'd do. Then I'd put every single dollar into Facebook Ads because I still think that's the best place to put your money until you get to a point where the money is better spent on something else. All you need is an amazing product, the ability to make content, and Facebook Ads."

The Four Phases of the Codex

What Sean describes is a phase-one brand, and the approach he describes is perfect for creating some serious momentum right out of the gate. Phase one is the launch phase; it's all about launching, getting your proof of concept validated, and gaining some initial traction. A phase-one brand has one solid asset for generating attention, such as Facebook ads; one asset for effectively demonstrating value, like a website complete with CRO best practices and piles of social proof; and one monetization asset, such as a flagship offer that people can't resist buying.

But what happens when Zuckerberg pushes an update that causes your business manager to bug out and your Facebook Ad Account to be shut down for a month? Your entire business shuts down; that's what happens. Trust me; I know from experience.

When Dan and I felt like our business was ripping and nothing could hurt us, we failed to realize that even though we were making $600,000 a month, we were still only in phase one of the Codex. As a result, we were vulnerable as a business. Because we had only one attention asset, when that asset—our Facebook ads—crashed, everything downstream also began to suffer.

As you can see, scaling revenue above and beyond what is appropriate for your infrastructure and the phase you're in is extremely dangerous. Often, the further you scale beyond what your phase can support, the more at risk you are, and the faster your business will go up in flames should one of those assets stop working.

According to the Codex, healthy growth would suggest that at around the $100,000-a-month mark, a brand should begin planning a transition into phase two. This involves adding one additional asset to each of the three categories: attention, demonstration, and monetization. The sequence in which these additional assets are implemented and validated is less important than creating balance within the Codex across all three layers. It's okay for your Codex to be lopsided during the transition from one phase to the next. However, it's crucial to avoid a situation where you keep adding assets in one layer, such as having four assets for attention but only one for demonstration and one for monetization.

In my experience, although many people don't precisely know why they fear their sales are going to fall apart, they almost intuitively sense that something is off. Most of these people have fairly successful phase-one brands. When we present the full breakdown of the Codex to them and begin strategically transitioning to a phase that's appropriate for them—while also planning for the next phase—it's as if a weight is lifted from their chests.

But that's not even the best part, and it's not why I love the Codex so much. We often see glass ceilings shattered, with brands suddenly stepping off the plateau they've been stuck on and advancing to new levels.

We're currently working with a men's outdoor brand. When we began our work together, they were doing about $40,000 a month using Facebook ads and a Shopify store selling individual products. A few optimizations to this phase-one strategy and better ad creative quickly moved them above $100k a month, at which point we transitioned into phase two by adding paid search in the form of Google ads as an additional attention asset and a fully built email and SMS strategy to better nurture and demonstrate value to the customer. We also began using special offers in addition to individual product sales to unlock more monetization opportunities. Once these were locked in and revenue had grown to $400,000 a month, we transitioned into phase three.

In the third phase, we added TikTok as another source of paid social traffic. However, since we already had Facebook ads, this didn't technically count as another attention asset, so the brand also doubled down on organic efforts by creating a YouTube channel and committing to more consistent organic posting across Facebook, Instagram, and TikTok.

The next demonstration asset we added was on-platform shops for Meta and TikTok, which was fantastic because sales continued to come in through these shops even when the Shopify store was experiencing issues. Lastly, as a result of increased visibility through strong attention assets, the brand had also been securing several wholesale relationships. These relationships began providing an entirely new stream of revenue, completely unrelated to the online store.

By following the principles of the Codex, over the course of about four years, this brand went from $480,000 a year to $25,000,000 when you include wholesale revenue. And guess what? They experienced all kinds of trouble, including imitators scamming people with knock-off sites, ad account issues, and worse-than-expected results from time to time, but their progress never stopped. No investors, no outside cash, just a young guy with awesome products and a dream, taking the right incremental steps. They are currently planning a transition from phase three to phase four and have goals of getting to $100,000,000 over the next five years.

The Codex offers a strategic blueprint for navigating the complexities of digital retail. Its holistic approach to brand awareness, product demonstration and nurturing, and monetization paves the way for DTC brands to achieve scalable growth, market differentiation, operational efficiency, and durability. By embracing and customizing the Codex to their unique business models, DTC brands can not only survive but flourish in a very competitive digital marketplace, securing their place as industry leaders and innovators.

Sales Consistency

Before we end this chapter, I want to zoom way out and ask a simple yet powerful question: Why do we want sales consistency in the first place? We desire sales consistency because revenue is the lifeblood of a business, and we are hardwired for survival.

Earlier in the chapter, I mentioned that humans have some form of the following basic needs: purpose, understanding, belonging, security, significance, and love. However, what's even more foundational than these is the unconscious biological urge to survive. Psychologist Carl Jung said, "Until you make the unconscious conscious, it will direct your life, and you will call it fate."

It's a fact that your sales will dip, and you will experience hard times. Bulletproofing your sales isn't about trying to avoid this reality but about strategically building the infrastructure needed to raise the valleys and capitalize on the peaks so the dips are less impactful, allowing you to remain in the fight. When you do experience dips, just remember that nothing ever moves in a straight line. When the unconscious urge to survive screams at you to freak out and be anxious, you can move past it, knowing that it's just your body doing its thing, trying to protect you.

Key Takeaways:

- **Complex Systems:** Sales challenges often arise from multiple small issues within the system. By understanding that every system is designed to yield specific results, it's possible to redesign for better outcomes.

- **The Codex Framework:** The Codex, comprising three main components (attention, demonstration, and monetization), offers a blueprint for scalable and sustainable growth. Each component is crucial for attracting customers, showcasing the brand and products, and generating revenue.

- **Phased Growth:** The Codex suggests a phased approach to implementing growth strategies. Starting with one solid asset in each category, brands should expand their assets as they grow, aiming for a balanced and robust marketing system.

- **Components of the Codex:**

    - **Attention:** Diverse strategies like paid social, paid search, organic, and outbound efforts to capture customer interest.

    - **Demonstration:** Assets like websites, special offer pages, and on-platform shops to showcase products and brand value.

    - **Monetization:** Tactics for converting interest into sales, including offers, product sales, wholesale, repeat purchases, and brick-and-mortar retail.

- **Survival and Basic Needs:** Beyond business strategies, the chapter touches on the foundational human needs driving the pursuit of sales consistency, including survival, purpose, belonging, and significance.

- **Facing Challenges:** Challenges in business will inevitably arise. It's important to have a strategic, well-structured approach to mitigating their impact and ensuring resilience.

CHAPTER 7

Commanding Attention and Building an Endless Ocean of Traffic

People spend an average of seven and a half hours per day online, swiping, scrolling, tapping, and clicking. This means there has never been a better time in history to get in front of your customers and scale your store to six or seven figures per month than now.

Facebook boasts more than three billion monthly active users, TikTok has over 1.6 billion users, and there are over 8.5 billion searches on Google every single day. Hungry people are constantly scouring the World Wide Web for solutions to their problems. All you have to do is get in front of them.

The most consistent and scalable way to generate wealth is by turning ad dollars into profit. Certainly, there are many other ways to generate traffic to your store and eventually convert it, but buying shoutouts, influencer marketing, blogs, SEO, and giveaways all take a backseat to the ability to run ads and convert them into profit. Honestly, many of these other traffic-generation tactics are only successful when used within or paired with a proper paid ads strategy.

So, how do we do it? How do we command the attention of our audience and tap into an endless ocean of traffic that we will then convert into paying customers? Most people believe it's by having all the right settings in their ad account, prioritizing tactical button-pushing above having a solid traffic strategy with a message that actually attracts people.

Ten years ago, there was so much opportunity with paid ads that simply knowing how to target an audience that was semi-interested in what you had to offer worked because the competition was much lower. By simply showing up, people would get sales no matter how mediocre the content of their ads was.

During this era, when we were working with some of our first clients, I remember we had a client who had one of the most random ecommerce stores I had ever seen. They sold blinged-out belt buckles, cowboy boots, battery chargers, LED light bars for big trucks, and tattered baseball caps with catchy slogans on them. The site was ugly; they had no social media presence, a tiny online sales history and existing customer base, and no data to draw insights from. But what happened next is something I will never forget.

We took an organic post of an awful product photo on a white background that had brought in a couple of sales and relaunched it to an interest-based audience on Facebook, and people went nuts over it. The product was a distressed baseball hat with the word "blessed" embroidered on the front, and the post simply read "#blessed." Month after month, this ad would bring in $40,000 of revenue as Midwest mom after Midwest mom gobbled it up. I think it's safe to say that this will likely never happen again.

As more and more people learned how to run ads and get in front of a somewhat targeted audience, more sophisticated ad strategists who knew how to "work the algorithm" had a competitive edge. They knew how to target better than anyone else, how to set up segmented retargeting stacks, and how to quickly obtain the necessary amount of impressions and conversion events needed to optimize and scale ads. As long as the brand provided a good product and content, they would have a high chance of success with this system.

This way of doing things has been obsolete for a long time. We are in an entirely new age, the age of AI, and sadly, even though that competitive edge is all but gone, there are still people trying to optimize the old system and wondering why they can't get good returns and their competition is running circles around them.

In the new age of advertising, no one has a tactical advantage because artificial intelligence has taken over, performing much better than any human ever could. This truth will only become more evident as time progresses. Certainly, it still pays to have someone who knows how to set up ads properly and structure marketing efforts in a way that maximizes the likelihood of success, but for the most part, the playing field has been leveled.

The new competitive edge now lies in what people see, read, and hear. In the past, managing the ad account correctly and generating enough impressions could help a brand with a mediocre strategy achieve satisfactory results. Today, this is far from the truth.

The truth is, victory isn't won in the ad account; it's won through a blend of human psychology and viral, top-converting formats. Victory is achieved by integrating information, which can only be found by empathetically walking in the shoes of your dream customer, into age-old frameworks known to convert yet tailored to current trends. Victory is won by understanding your customers better than anyone else and communicating with them in a way that resonates while also keeping your approach fresh. Why? Because people hate ads. Most ads are as unexciting as ordering plain vanilla ice cream with no toppings in the finest gourmet ice cream shop in the world.

This is why the world's top brands invest massive amounts to hire the best advertising minds to create their campaigns.

Imagine if you could have these same experts crafting ads for your business. How much would that be worth to you?

Well, here's some great news: you don't need to become an advertising master or spend a fortune hiring top-tier experts to create high-converting ads for your brand.

Why? Because their most successful work is public, and we can see which ads they invest the most in and which perform best. Even better, our team has spent nearly a decade analyzing and reverse-engineering these top-performing ads, investing over $100,000,000.00 to test and refine these formats. We've turned this knowledge into always-updated, easy-to-use formats just for you

It's not enough to go into ads manager, upload some product photos, perhaps a bit of user-generated content (UGC), write some basic, generic copy that people have seen a million times, and then sprinkle some emojis on it and hope it converts.

As an alternative, here are twelve ad formats that we have used to generate hundreds of millions of dollars. It's not just us; brands like AG1, True Classic Tees, and Gymshark are using these formats as well to achieve even greater success and consistently outmaneuver the market.

You don't need to obsess over the right bid cap, click optimization, and a hundred different attribution windows. You need to create ads and hooks that are so different, funny, and unique that people simply cannot look away or help themselves from clicking. On any given day, you're competing with DMs,

TikTok, a lot of beautiful but barely dressed women on Instagram, podcasters, and earth-shattering headlines on the news. So, unless you instantly hook your customer, the show's over.

By using the ad formats provided below, you can streamline the process of finding top-performing ads for your brand, saving you the significant time and financial investment usually needed to discover and validate these strategies on your own.

Top-Performing Ad Formats

- **The ThumbStopper Ad:** Designed to be visually captivating and instantly engaging, this ad format uses striking visuals or unexpected elements to make viewers pause while scrolling. Use it to grab attention quickly, ideally within the first few seconds, to intrigue and draw viewers into your message or product offering. ThumbStopper ads are especially effective for creating a strong first impression and increasing brand awareness.

- **The Product Highlight Ad:** This format, though very common, converts very well because it educates the customer so well. Product highlight ads showcase key features or unique selling points of a specific product. Use them to draw attention to the special aspects of a product that set it apart from competitors.

- **Product Features:** Similar to product highlights, but focus more on the detailed characteristics and specifications of a product. Use them to educate potential customers about the product's specific benefits and functionalities.

- **User-Generated Content (UGC):** Harness the power of content produced by influencers, creators, and customers, such as reviews or photos featuring your product. This approach embodies the principle that people buy from people. UGC fosters trust and authenticity by highlighting genuine user experiences and satisfaction with your products in real-life scenarios.

- **Comparison (Us vs. Them):** Highlight the differences between your products and competitors in a side-by-side comparison. Use this format to emphasize your product's superior features, quality, or value.

- **Lifestyle (Problem Solved):** Showcase your product within a lifestyle context, illustrating how it solves a specific problem or improves the customer's life. This format helps potential buyers visualize the product in use and understand its real-world application.

- **Testimonial Comment Screenshot:** Use screenshots of positive customer testimonials or reviews, especially those shared on social media. This format leverages social proof to build credibility and trust with your audience.

- **Pain-Point Highlight:** Focus on a specific problem or challenge your target audience faces and show how your product provides the solution. This format resonates with the audience's needs and positions your product as the answer.

- **TikTok Comment Reply:** Engage with your audience by creating ads that mimic the style of responding to comments on TikTok (or any other platform for that matter). This format is great for interaction and feels personalized and engaging.

- **Big Percentage Sale Announcement:** Announce major sales or discounts with a focus on the percentage saved. This format creates urgency and appeals to deal-seekers.

- **UGC Bestseller Carousel:** Create a carousel of your best-selling products, but showcase them using user-generated content. This format allows potential customers to see popular products and real customer adoption in one ad.

- **Dynamic Product Ad Carousels:** Though these are pretty straightforward, you do not want to sleep on them because, time and time again, we have seen these kinds of ads not only be top performers in the account but also top performers for very long periods of time. So what are they, and why do they work so well? They are dynamically populated ads that pull information directly from your Shopify store into a carousel and update automatically.

- These are great evergreen ads because they dynamically adjust based on things like what the individual meta user might be most interested in according to their online shopping behavior, what's in stock and what's not, what's trending in the marketplace, and many other things. They're easy to build, and they always stay updated.

In one of my all-time favorite books, *Breakthrough Advertising: How to Write Ads That Shatter Traditions and Sales Records*, copywriting legend Eugene Schwartz states:

"Copy cannot create desire for a product. It can only take the hopes, dreams, fears, and desires that already exist in the hearts of millions of people and focus those already existing desires onto a particular product. This is the copywriter's task: not to create this mass desire—but to channel and direct it."

So, what happens when you do this well? You end up with tons of engagement, cheap CPMs and CPCs, better conversion rates, cheaper CPAs, and optimal ROAS. There's no need to reinvent the wheel, no need to waste your valuable time, and no need to burn up your hard-earned money testing random ideas.

I used to dislike the idea of relying on frameworks and certainly wasn't eager to use templates. Like most entrepreneurs, I have a creative side, and I genuinely enjoy the process of generating new and innovative ideas. However, over time, I discovered that having frameworks actually empowered me to be more creative and generate more ideas because they provided a starting point.

I now know these formats and frameworks so well that ideas spontaneously come to me as I go about my day. While driving down the road, I might have five ideas for the local business I just passed. When I sit down intentionally to come up with ideas, the floodgates open because I no longer have to struggle through the initial phase of getting started. The icing on the cake is that all these ideas bear a close resemblance to ones that are currently generating a lot of money.

Key Takeaways:

- **Unprecedented Access to Customers:** With billions of active users across platforms like Facebook, TikTok, and Google, businesses have unparalleled opportunities to reach potential customers.

- **Primacy of Paid Ads:** Among various traffic generation tactics, paid advertising is the most direct and scalable way to convert ad spend into profit.

- **Evolution of Advertising:** The landscape of online advertising has shifted from simple targeting techniques to sophisticated strategies leveraging AI, making traditional methods obsolete.

- **The Importance of Creative Strategy:** In an era where AI levels the tactical playing field, the competitive edge shifts to creative content that resonates with human psychology and viral trends.

- **Engagement Over Tactics:** Successful advertising today relies more on engaging and unique content than on tactical ad account management.

- **Innovative Ad Formats:** The chapter outlines ten high-converting ad formats, including ThumbStopper ads, product highlights, user-generated content, and lifestyle problem-solved formats, tailored to captivate audiences and drive conversions.

- **Leveraging Trends:** Tools like Google Trends and TikTok's Creative Center can infuse current trends into these ad formats for fresher, more relevant content.

- **Continuous Testing and Refreshing:** The key to sustained success is in the ongoing testing of new creatives and refreshing ad content to keep pace with trends and audience preferences.

- **Copywriting Wisdom:** To echo Eugene Schwartz, effective copywriting channels existing desires onto a product rather than creating new desires.

- **Efficiency Through Frameworks:** Frameworks and templates for ad content can empower creativity, providing a foundation from which to develop innovative ideas without starting from scratch.

CHAPTER 8

Multiplying Returns With the Right AOV Strategy

"Would you like fries with that?"

Those six little words make McDonald's most of its profit. When you think about the golden arches, you probably think of the Big Mac or the cheeseburger, but McDonald's pride and joy is actually its fries. Why? Their profit margin for fries is between 75–90%, almost double what they make on burgers. This story plays itself out across many industries, not just fast food restaurants.

What's the point? That same idea can and should be brought into your ecommerce store. When you create easy-to-grab upsell offers in your purchase process, you can drastically increase AOV, liquidate more ad costs, and create new dimensions of growth that would've never been there before because the thing that stops most people from scaling hard is the fact that the return they're getting doesn't generate enough cash to fund it.

After your ads generate massive amounts of high-quality traffic, the next step toward growth is to increase your AOV through upsells. To put it plainly, before we explore methods to increase AOV, let's address why AOV is crucial for maximizing your marketing investment returns.

AOV's significance lies in the fact that although the cost to acquire a customer (CAC) is variable, it doesn't directly correlate with the average order value. Acquiring a customer for a $600 product typically costs more than for a $60 product. However, offering a product at $8.99 doesn't guarantee low acquisition costs. In simpler terms, a lower-priced product doesn't automatically lead to a lower CAC. Conversely, enhancing your AOV through upsells doesn't necessarily increase your CAC. This principle forms the foundation of the strategy I'm about to share.

Currently, our average CAC across all the brands we manage is somewhere in the neighborhood of $26–31. If our client's AOV was around $50, that would be okay, especially with added repeat purchases enhancing the LTV. However, when we worked to increase the AOV to an average of $97 for these brands, the returns significantly improved, putting more profit in the pockets of our clients.

Numerous strategies exist to achieve this. Recently, a team member shared an experience where they enhanced a client's AOV from $89 to $198 simply by installing a simple "Frequently Bought Together" app on Shopify. This app displays complementary clothing items alongside what a user adds to their shopping cart, remarkably improving the client's AOV without negatively impacting their CAC, thereby significantly enhancing returns as effortlessly as flipping a switch.

Another client of ours, who also runs a women's boutique but who also offers children's clothing, adopted a similar approach. But this time, instead of using an app to suggest complementary items, they implemented a dynamic "Mommy and Me" popup. This popup displays matching children's outfits corresponding to the item just added to the cart and offers a slight discount when you purchase the matching set. The take rate was awesome. Many buyers now purchase two outfits instead of one, thereby increasing the AOV and boosting the ROI.

Our team conducts hundreds of store audits each year. During these audits, we meticulously analyze and break stores down, including brand positioning, ad creative, traffic sources, website design, emails, etc., providing brand owners with a clear and simplified pathway toward growth (our motto, after all, is "Growth Made Simple").

One of the most common mistakes we see is that after discovering the brand has been running just some basic ads, nothing like the ones described in the previous chapter, they add insult to injury by directing traffic to either a bland product page or, even worse, to their homepage.

In a marketplace chock full of online sellers, people are being swarmed with lame ads selling cheesy products. If you really want to establish your brand, you simply cannot be like the side hustle Shopify store dropshipping questionable products from Alibaba. At one point, people could do this and make a few bucks, but that doesn't work anymore.

You need something entirely different: a strategy that not only creates an endless ocean of high-quality traffic to your store, boosts your AOV, and multiplies your ROI but also keeps the customers that you already paid to acquire coming back for more with each purchase, adding to that lifetime value and making your store more profitable. Once you have that, everything improves. Your traffic becomes cheaper, your conversion rates improve, AOVs skyrocket, and as a result, your overall returns increase, which means you can afford to increase ad spend, boost sales volume, and hire people to run the business while you take up pickleball and sip cocktails.

When it comes to first-time customers, most people will buy one of your cheapest products to test you out. This makes it almost impossible to scale your ads because the return just isn't high enough to support any meaningful scale. If you're working with a basic, bare-bones Shopify site, you'll find that your AOVs are disappointingly low, and your traffic is a mere trickle. This is normally because each time you attempt to scale your ad spend, your ROAS takes a dive. The root of the issue? Often, the AOVs simply aren't high enough to effectively reach and scale to cold audiences that become fatigued after just a small amount of ad spend.

Sending your traffic to a basic product page that only offers short, descriptive copy is not enough to convert visitors into customers. This approach only provides them with the basic features of your product, which might suffice for someone who has already decided to search for and buy your product. This approach caters only to individuals who are already aware of their needs and are simply comparing solutions. Alarmingly, this segment of the market makes up just 3% of all potential customers, and it's quickly exhausted. Relying solely on this way of doing things limits your growth potential. No matter how many creative ad ideas you test or new angles you introduce, you won't be able to scale effectively.

Here's a better, more lucrative alternative. After someone clicks on our ads, direct them to a jaw-dropping product page with copy that does more than just list the features of the product. Yes, it provides all the necessary information to empower the shopper to make an educated purchase, but it also glistens, gleams, and paints a picture of how this product will improve their lives.

On this page, we initiate the AOV-boosting process. The initial part of this process aims to secure a purchase. We might also increase the AOV in this first step, but the primary goal is to get customers to enter their credit card digits and buy.

Below, in no specific order, is a list of our top-performing offers that can be used in step one of the AOV-boosting process.

Boosting AOV: Step 1 – Securing the Purchase With an Offer

Free Shipping Thresholds

Free shipping thresholds are a tactic where free shipping is offered to customers once their order value meets or exceeds a specified amount. This approach encourages customers to add more items to their cart to qualify for free shipping, effectively increasing the AOV. It's a win-win situation: customers feel they're getting a good deal by saving on shipping costs, and retailers enjoy higher sales volumes.

Example: A bookstore might set a free shipping threshold of $50. A customer with a cart total of $45 is incentivized to add another book to their order to avoid shipping fees.

Quantity Breaks

This is probably our favorite offer. Unlike free shipping thresholds, which unlock free delivery once an order meets a certain value, quantity breaks reward customers with greater discounts for buying in larger quantities. This strategy incentivizes customers to add more items to their cart. Even though people are getting a discount, they are buying a lot more of your product, effectively boosting the average AOV.

Example: A clothing retailer might implement a quantity break offer such as "Buy two, get 10% off. Buy three, get 15% off.

Buy four or more, get 20% off." A customer initially planning to purchase only one t-shirt might be tempted to buy three instead to get the 15% discount.

Buy One, Get One Free (BOGO)

This offer boosts sales volume by offering an additional item for free, enticing customers to purchase more.

Example: A skincare products store employs a BOGO deal on select creams, motivating customers to buy in bulk.

Free Gifts With Purchase

A complimentary gift with purchase increases the perceived value of buying, making deals more enticing.

Example: Purchases over $75 at a beauty store come with a free sample kit, encouraging higher spend and creating opportunities for future purchases of the products sampled.

Limited-Edition Products

Offering products in limited quantities creates a sense of exclusivity and urgency to buy.

Example: For Valentine's Day, an artisanal chocolate shop introduces a limited-edition flavor.

Interactive Offers

Personalized discounts or product recommendations through quizzes or interactive tools.

Example: A fitness store uses a quiz to recommend workout gear tailored to the customer and offers discounts on those recommendations.

Seasonal or Thematic Promotions

Offer promotions according to current events, seasons, or holidays.

Example: Leading up to summer, a home décor store discounts outdoor furniture, capitalizing on seasonal demand.

Flash Sales

Flash sales generate a sense of urgency by offering deals for a clearly listed limited time, encouraging quick customer action.

Example: A swimwear store initiates a 24-hour flash sale with 30% off all items to kickstart summer sales and efficiently clear out inventory.

Offer Stacking

Offer stacking is when you combine two or more offers. Typically, your landing page is built with a focus on one main offer, and then, as the checkout process is initiated, you do offer stacking as a pre-purchase order bump, cross-sell, or upsell.

Example: You go to your favorite athletic wear shop for their 30% off Fourth of July sale. When you add a pair of shoes to your cart, a pop-up window informs you that if you spend just $30 more dollars to put your cart value above $150, you will also get a free pair of American flag socks.

Boosting AOV: Step 2 – Post-Purchase Upsells

Let's assume you've followed all the concepts laid out in this book so far. You have a clear vision, and you know your numbers. You've mastered the art of brand building and are properly positioned against your competitors. You have amazing ads that drive traffic to your store, and now, thanks to a gorgeous landing page with an irresistible offer, your conversion rate is higher than ever, and people are consistently purchasing. You'd be pretty set, right? This is where the average Joe would stop, but I'm guessing you're not reading this in hopes of unlocking average results.

After someone enters their credit card information, checks out, and buys, we're just getting started. In the second step of the AOV-boosting process, we run them through a post-purchase upsell path. Brands that don't have this in place are likely leaving massive amounts of profits untouched on the table. Even some of the biggest, baddest brands out there aren't doing this.

Immediately after a customer completes the checkout but right before they reach the thank-you page, we present them with another irresistible offer, further increasing the likelihood of a larger AOV. Here, we can offer them more of what they just bought at a discount, complementary products, or even options like VIP processing, express shipping, warranties, and other easy-to-deliver, profit-boosting products and services, all with the single click of a button. That's the key. The beauty of a one-click upsell is that customers don't have to re-enter their payment details again. They simply click, and it's done.

"My ROAS isn't high enough" is the number one reason I hear for a brand's inability to scale hard. While this is often true, the issue usually lies in the fact that they're pulling the wrong lever in hopes of achieving a higher return. Yes, your ads need to be properly set up and managed, but an equally significant opportunity for brands to multiply their returns and generate more cash lies in increasing their AOV.

Many people invest time and money into improving their ads because they're not generating enough capital to support aggressive scaling. However, the real issue usually isn't that their cost to acquire a customer is too high. In fact, many brands are not far off our average of $26–31, which is entirely reasonable for acquiring a customer from a cold audience. The crux of the matter is that their AOVs are simply not high enough.

I've witnessed a lot of people thinking that premium brands don't run sales or promotions, and this is simply not true. Take Lululemon, for example. They are certainly not known for running sales, but a simple Google search will show you that you can buy overstocked items at a discounted price and even purchase slightly used Lululemon products at a discount as well. These sales do not steal from the perception of value and prestige that Lululemon carries; if anything, they make it stronger. Their products are still worthy of purchase after they've been used, which is a testament to their quality. It is possible to run special promotions and sales without coming off as a "discount brand."

Scaling your brand isn't just about attracting eyeballs through flashy ads or having the most cutting-edge product on the market. It's about strategically increasing your average order value to unlock levels of profitability that can transform your business from just surviving to thriving in a competitive marketplace.

Key Takeaways:

- **Leveraging High-Margin Upsells:** Like McDonald's offering fries with every purchase, focus on products or services with high profit margins as upsell opportunities to boost AOV.

- **Incorporating Strategic Offers**: Use offers such as free shipping thresholds, quantity breaks, and BOGO deals to incentivize higher spending, mirroring the strategic approaches that have doubled AOVs for our clients.

- **Offer Stacking and Post-Purchase Upsells**: Implement offer stacking during the checkout process, as well as post-purchase upsells, to further enhance AOV and customer lifetime value, ensuring every transaction maximizes potential revenue.

- **Understanding Your Market:** Recognize that most customers start with lower-priced items to test the brand. Using strategic upsells and improving product pages can convert these initial tests into lucrative, ongoing customer relationships.

- **The Power of Presentation:** A compelling product page that does more than list features -- one that paints a vivid picture of the product's impact on the customer's life— can significantly increase conversion rates and AOV.

Remember, the average Joe stops after achieving a basic level of success, but you're not aiming for average. You're setting your sights higher. With the right strategies to increase your AOV, as detailed in this chapter, you're well on your way to unlocking not just growth but exponential growth that can sustain your business long-term and allow you to enjoy the fruits of your labor.

Implementing these strategies requires a shift in focus from merely attracting traffic to maximizing the value of every customer interaction. As you move forward, keep these key takeaways in mind and consider how you can apply them to your store. By doing so, you'll not only increase your AOV but also set your brand apart in a crowded marketplace, ensuring a brighter, more profitable future.

CHAPTER 9

LTV Alchemy: Eight-Figure Customer Retention Secrets

Now, it's time to learn where the real money is made. In Chapter 7, we discussed how to leverage trends and top-performing ad concepts to capture boatloads of attention. Then, in Chapter 8, we learned how to turn casual shoppers into excited buyers with irresistible offers and product pages that not only convert but do so with the highest possible AOV, effectively multiplying the return on marketing dollars. Having exerted every effort possible to achieve the highest return in the customer acquisition process, our next step is to focus on enhancing the customers' lifetime value. This is where the real money is made.

So, what does this look like? For starters, depending on the industry, product type, and purchasing cycle, a healthy repeat purchase rate should be somewhere in the neighborhood of 30–40%. Obviously, the difference between a subscription-based business or a fast-moving consumer goods brand will be drastically different from a brand selling flagship products like "the only pair of jeans you will ever need." Regardless of the product or niche, maximizing customer lifetime value is the cornerstone of any great ecommerce strategy, and we achieve this by having a series of repeat-purchase nurturing systems that follow our front-end customer acquisition efforts.

Instead of doing the same boring old thing everyone else does, where we just send a simple thank-you email and then a discount code, hoping the customer buys again, we do things differently. We don't want to approach such a great opportunity casually and miss out, but we also don't want to overwhelm people with offer after offer until they unsubscribe and start to resent us for spamming their inboxes. Instead, we personalize every post-purchase journey and maximize each step for value.

When crafting these follow-up touch points, every detail is considered: how they heard about us, when they bought, what they bought, where they live, whether they have bought from us in the past, their gender, whether they prefer emails or texts, how often they want to hear from us—the list goes on. We curate every journey to the individual person. We make sure every step of the journey feels special and just for them. We focus on being helpful and engaging and on teaching customers about the products. We want to make them feel super happy about their purchase by showing them ways to make the best use of what they bought.

For example, if they purchased kitchen gadgets from us, we wouldn't stop at the sale. We would send them a series of recipes and how-to videos demonstrating how to easily prepare delicious meals. It's not just about the product; it's about enriching their experience. If we're selling yoga mats or fitness gear, we might share a variety of stretching and exercise routines suited to different skill levels. The goal of these first pieces of content is to ensure that our customers feel excited, supported, and informed, not bombarded or merely sold to.

This approach, which prioritizes giving customers value over asking for another purchase, fosters trust and cultivates long-term relationships. By encouraging people to use the products they've just purchased, you're establishing a strong connection. A lot of brands devote all their time and energy to front-end marketing and winning over potential buyers with their ads, which isn't bad in itself. However, if they fail to continue this effort or even take it up a notch post-purchase, they're missing out on tons of opportunities to engage with the people who love and support the brand the most by continuing to add value after the sale.

Doing this correctly takes an average brand that's just getting by and propels it directly into the big leagues because, in business, the one who can afford to spend the most to acquire a customer ultimately wins. While others go slow and play small, trying to make all their money on the first purchase, you'll be miles ahead, scaling aggressively because you understand that in 60 or 90 days, your return on marketing dollars will be even better than what you earned on the initial purchase value, thanks to all those repeat purchases coming through the door.

We love getting high returns on acquisition and do so regularly. However, remember that setting a high day-one ROAS as your North Star can sometimes restrict sales volume and actually lead to lower overall profits. My goal in sharing all this information here is to inform you and present you with options. Once people see the math, they usually opt for more profit. From what we've seen, very few get this right, but the ones who do are dominating. They understand that buying ads on platforms like Google, Meta, and TikTok is an auction, and they are buying up all the customers on these platforms because they can afford to, as their LTV is so strong. And they win over and over and over again.

Be honest. Have you ever made a purchase only to find out that, as a "thank you," you've been granted lifetime access to a relentless stream of spam in your inbox? Being added to an email list, especially after making a purchase, should feel special. The secret to increasing LTV isn't bombarding your list with as many emails as possible; it's about making your subscribers feel lucky to be there.

No one wants to feel like they're just another contact for your all-too-often sales pushes. Being on your list should carry perks, such as exclusive discounts. Perhaps it means customers get early access to new products or sales events before the general public. Small things like this transform the email list experience from a burden to a privilege.

You're not just selling a product; you're guiding customers to a valuable experience. Once they are satisfied and engaged, we transition from exclusively adding value to introducing repeat-purchase, upsell, and cross-sell opportunities.

Here is a 50,000-foot view of some of our favorite programs and offers that we tastefully introduce and use to increase LTV and customer loyalty for DTC brands.

Loyalty Programs

A well-structured loyalty program is more than just a points system; it's a powerful tool that makes interacting with your brand feel like a game. Loyalty programs encourage repeat purchases and deepen customer engagement in a fun and exciting way. By offering exclusive rewards, discounts, or early access to new products, brands can make customers feel valued and incentivized to continue their patronage. This not only boosts LTV but also transforms occasional buyers into brand advocates.

"Subscribe and Save" Offers

Subscription models have revolutionized the way consumers interact with brands. By offering a "subscribe and save" option, DTC brands can ensure a steady stream of revenue while providing convenience and value to their customers. This model encourages consistent engagement, as customers look forward to their regular deliveries, and it also simplifies the repurchase process, enhancing customer retention and LTV. This offer works exceptionally well for consumable products, such as food, beverages, beauty supplies, or anything else that gets used up over time and then needs to be replenished.

True Subscription-Based Businesses

While "subscribe and save" options provide a convenient way for customers to make repeat purchases and get a discount, a true subscription-based model goes much deeper, fundamentally changing the relationship between a brand and its customer base. At the heart of the subscription model is the ability to generate predictable, recurring revenue. This stability allows businesses to plan for the future with greater confidence, investing in innovation, expansion through marketing, customer service, and other growth initiatives with a clear understanding of their financial trajectory. Unlike the "subscribe and save" model, which hinges on the customer's need or desire to replenish, a subscription service offers a continuous value proposition that keeps the revenue flowing.

In October 2020, we began collaborating with a brand that sells literature-based subscription boxes. Each month, avid readers receive an exclusive luxe edition of a beloved novel, along with items curated and inspired by that month's theme. This brand not only effectively created recurring revenue from each customer acquired but also built a powerful community of fiction readers—a place where people who enjoy sitting by a candle, drinking a cup of tea, and cracking open their next adventure feel at home. They increased their monthly revenue from just over $100,000 to well over a million dollars a month in just three short years, consistently reaching $1.4 to $1.8 million each month in year four.

As the guy blessed to be helping with the marketing, I cannot applaud this brand more or think of a better way to propel a company into the $10-million-and-above club than by leveraging the revenue consistency and strong LTVs of a subscription-based ecommerce brand. Brands that effectively retain their customers in this model can afford to pay more for customer acquisition, be more aggressive with their marketing, plan more easily, and scale with consistency. The real icing on the cake, however, is that now, with a massive group of die-hard customers, they can also do exclusive one-time product drops that often sell out in a matter of days. We've even seen $600,000 come in from a single email in just a few hours.

Community Engagement Programs

Understanding that it's not all about you is the foundation of strong community engagement programs. This might sound funny, but I see lots of people overestimating their own allure. They commit the deadly mistake of assuming it's solely about their perceived coolness or the excellence of their products. They believe that putting out the right image will draw people into their orbit, transforming them into followers, loyal customers, and brand advocates. This is not the case at all. The brands that truly spark movements are those that position the customer as the hero.

Imagine if Nike constantly bragged about their products and how superior they were to other brands. What if their slogan was "We Did It" instead of "Just Do It"? It would never work. Nike inspires its customers to believe in their potential for greatness.

The "Just Do It" slogan perfectly encapsulates this ethos. Nike tells a story where the customer is at the center of its own narrative of perseverance, determination, and triumph. Nike's marketing campaigns feature athletes of all levels, from the novice embarking on their first run to the professional striving for a world title, reinforcing the idea that in every person lies the potential to overcome obstacles and achieve greatness.

This approach transforms Nike's products from mere athletic gear into symbols of personal ambition and self-improvement. Customers are not just buying a pair of shoes; they're investing in a better version of themselves that believes in the possibility of "more"—more effort, more progress, more achievements.

Nike's ability to connect with the aspirations and emotions of its audience has not only made it a leader in the athletic apparel industry but has also fostered an engaged and passionate customer base that identifies deeply with what the brand stands for.

Case Study

Okay, so you might be thinking, *This is all good and dandy, but Nike has a lot of prestige. How could I ever create the same kind of engagement that would empower a program to keep people sticking around and spending money?* Let's take a look at a real-life case study as an example of how we approached this with one of our clients.

First, we started with the basics and asked, "What does our ideal customer want that we can help solve?"

The simple answer was: "High-quality, super-cute clothes."

But, to make the marketing powerful, we had to do what any good marketer does: take it a step further and ask, "Why?"

After extensive brainstorming, we hypothesized that the real reason a customer would purchase super-cute, high-quality clothes from this premium clothing brand for women was that they wanted to elevate their status—a desire as old as time itself. Bingo! That was something we could work with.

We then asked, "How do we make the customer the hero on their journey toward greater status?"

We came up with a gamified experience with the brand that moved the customer closer to the goal of being admired by their friends. Each step in the buyer's journey would simultaneously foster more engagement.

It went something like this. First, we provided more status, initially through the outfit, then through the potential of going viral, and finally, through the opportunity to become a sponsored influencer, which, by the way, is currently the most desired occupation among Gen Z.

Here's how the program works: first, buy an outfit you love; second, make a video of yourself, post it on TikTok, and tag the brand for a chance to go viral; third, unlock the potential of receiving an official brand sponsorship.

In this process, the customer is the hero and clearly sees how they can achieve what they want in a fun and engaging way. Meanwhile, the brand gets sales, acquires tons of UGC to fuel their ads, creates a social movement, builds an affiliate network, and increases the lifetime value of their customers.

Here is one version of the ad copy we used to promote this program:

"Guys, guys, GUYS!!!! My new [@brand_name outfit] went viral on TikTok and they just offered me a sponsorship!! I'm so excited!! All you have to do is get a super cute skirt and sweatshirt combo, then just upload a video like mine!! [yellow heart emoji] If you need me, I'll be over here, sponsored by [Brand Name] [sparkles emoji]."

As you can imagine, this has been a powerful addition to an already strong brand, and they are winning the hearts of thousands of customers.

Building a Community

Increasing LTV through community is all about creating spaces for customers to engage with the brand and each other, whether through forums, social media groups, or exclusive events. Being in a community creates a sense of belonging, which can significantly enhance customer loyalty, making individuals feel like they're part of something larger than just a transaction. As customers engage and form connections under the brand's umbrella, they are constantly exposed to lifetime value-increasing opportunities.

Continuously Improving Your Offerings

The pursuit of excellence in your product offerings is a never-ending journey that should be significantly driven by customer feedback. This iterative process of refining and improving your products based on customer feedback shows them that they are a valuable part of your business and gets them to stick around longer. It also ensures that the products remain high quality, reliable, and in tune with customer expectations. Such dedication to product excellence not only addresses the immediate needs of your customers but also fosters a sense of trust and reliability in your brand. When customers know that they can consistently rely on your products to meet or exceed their expectations, repeat business becomes a natural outcome, thereby boosting LTV.

Expand Product Lines

Parallel to improving existing products, introducing new products or variations plays a crucial role in catering to the evolving needs and desires of your customer base. By expanding your product lines, you demonstrate a commitment to growth and innovation, keeping your brand relevant and appealing in a competitive market. This approach not only attracts new customers but also offers existing customers more reasons to stay engaged with your brand. Whether it's through offering complimentary products, exploring new categories, or customizing products to meet niche demands, expanding your product lines ensures that your brand remains a constant in your customers' lives, further increasing their lifetime value to your business.

The journey from transaction to loyalty sets average brands apart from great ones. The key to unlocking significant profits lies not in mere tactics but in deepening customer relationships through valuable content, initiatives, and offers. By focusing on maximizing LTV through genuine engagement and value creation, brands can achieve sustainable growth and profitability.

Key Takeaways:

- **Focus on LTV:** Aim for a high repeat purchase rate to maximize LTV, adapting strategies to fit different industries and product types.

- **Personalize Post-Purchase Communication:** Tailor post-purchase interactions to individual customer profiles to enhance their experience.

- **Prioritize Value Before Upselling:** Offer genuine value to customers before introducing upsell and cross-sell opportunities to build trust and loyalty.

- **Implement Engaging Loyalty Programs:** Use loyalty programs to incentivize repeat purchases and deepen engagement with fun, exclusive rewards.

- **Leverage Subscription Models:** Subscription services ensure steady revenue and customer convenience, boosting retention and LTV.

- **Engage Your Customers**: Foster brand loyalty by positioning customers as heroes of their own stories and engaging them in meaningful ways.

- **Build and Nurture Communities:** Create digital and in-person meeting places for customer interaction to foster a sense of belonging and loyalty.

- **Iteratively Improve Products:** Use customer feedback to continuously refine products, ensuring quality and relevance.

- **Expand Product Lines:** Keep the brand relevant by introducing new and complementary products that meet evolving customer needs.

- **Transition from Transactions to Loyalty:** The ultimate goal is to deepen customer relationships through value-driven content and offers, setting the stage for sustainable growth and profitability.

CHAPTER 10

Putting It All Together

Having stood alongside hundreds of DTC brand founders in the ever-changing landscape of digital marketing, I've had the privilege and blessing of fighting for the realization of their dreams—to grow sales, achieve market dominance, and enjoy various personal freedoms. Trusted as the expert team, we've pushed their vision forward, becoming an extension of their brands, goals, and values.

As an active participant in helping many cross into eight-figure territory, I've been gifted with a clear picture of success—a deep view into what works and what doesn't. I've observed the commonalities between the one out of ten brands that scale and how they differ from the nine out of ten that fail. As we near the end of our journey together, I'd like to paint a picture of the potential that's waiting in the not-so-distant future for you.

What This All Means for Your Business

As Temu and Amazon ravage the online space with big budgets, spending billions of dollars to acquire customers at a loss in hopes of retaining them with price and convenience, you'll stand strong, charging a premium price with a brand that resonates at a deeper level. Your value proposition and the experience you provide will be specific to you and something these big companies can never replicate, steal, or compete with.

You'll have a crystal-clear vision that is so vivid and well-documented that simply sharing it with others brings powerful forces into motion, making your dreams a reality. With your goals clearly established, you'll be able to celebrate the small wins that compound over time and inch you closer to the life you want with a business that serves you instead of you being a slave to the business.

Setbacks won't bother you anymore. Instead, you will consider them steps in the right direction because the decisions you've made will still align with where you want to be. You've also done the work to identify your non-negotiables, ensuring that every new level of success you reach doesn't rob you or your family but creates more freedom and purpose for you.

You'll know the game of customer acquisition so well that, based on the economics of your products and marketing, you will no longer need difficult-to-achieve-and-maintain returns. And instead of getting lost in a sea of metrics that don't really matter and watching your bank account stand still or whither, you'll have defined your North Star metrics, allowing you to set the right KPIs to move you forward and keep a close pulse on the health of your business.

You'll be engineered for success and know exactly what needs to happen to turn a profit. And rather than hoping it all works out, you'll be able to look at the situation mathematically and simply do what needs to be done. You'll be able to look at data clearly and make simple yet powerful decisions.

Unlike the "poor brands" out there, you'll know exactly what it looks like to play at a higher level. You'll know the role ads play in your business and that what you're building can and will lead to real wealth creation. You'll also have systems in place to ensure that this happens, whether it be investments that grow and compound over time, funded by the success of your store, or a large exit opportunity.

Instead of watching campaign after campaign start strong and then flop, instead of getting stuck in cycles that never lead to more revenue and profit, you'll know exactly how to invest in your audience, build relationship equity, and tastefully run direct-response marketing to bring home the bacon without ever exhausting the goodwill you've worked so hard to build. The solutions you provide will be specific and resonate with the right people, and you'll be distinguished from your competitors. When people see your marketing, they will know without a doubt why they should buy from you.

When everyone else is riding the revenue roller coaster and bracing for the next big Apple, Meta, artificial intelligence, or Google disruption, you'll be solid as a rock, with multiple ways to drive attention to your brand and demonstrate value to your market. And you'll happily accept their money in exchange for the value you give them. Having your business built this way will not only provide you with durability, adaptability, and optionality, but it will literally give you peace and comfort and allow you to enjoy time off without worrying about it all falling apart.

Your ads will be absolute fire all the time. They will be relevant, they will be trendy, and they will be engineered for success and informed by the billions of dollars that other brands have already spent on testing. Yet each ad will be uniquely you and perfectly aligned with your brand. You won't create new ads out of desperation as sales are tanking because you have to; you'll be leading the charge with new ads at a comfortable cadence that always keeps things fresh.

As your competitors slam their heads against the wall, trying to lower the cost of acquiring customers, you'll be playing with levers that they didn't even consider. You'll constantly use industry-leading methods to increase your average order value and thus get way higher returns, even though your cost to acquire a customer didn't actually go down.

There will be a steady stream of customers coming through the door every month who are falling deeper and deeper in love with your products. Each piece of content they receive, even after the initial purchase, will make them even more committed to your business, occasionally to the point of them becoming brand ambassadors for you and adding more momentum into your marketing inertia, creating the snowball effect. This growing affinity for your brand will result in more repeat purchase activity and bolster your LTV, allowing your brand to experience higher degrees of profitability over time.

After all this, you will feel happy because you built your business the right way and didn't sacrifice your life on the altar of monetary success. Instead, you built your brand in such a way that it made your life and the lives of those around you much better. You'll have freedom over your time, allowing you to engage in activities you enjoy and believe in. You'll have freedom over your money, seeing the potential to earn without limits based on the magnitude of problems you solve and living free from constant financial worries. You'll have freedom of relationship, with the privilege to choose whom you spend your time with and whom you do business with, prioritizing mutual respect and appreciation. And you'll have freedom of purpose, making your work more than just a job but a means to empower your core values and ideals, providing a profound sense of purpose in your life.

Sounds amazing, right? But that's not even the best part. Much of what you learned in this book is based on principles that have consistently stood the test of time and endured many earth-shaking disruptions. In fact, a lot of what is written here was learned and validated not by me but by marketers who sold products in the newspaper with one tiny headline and a small body of ad copy.

Billions of newspapers later and after countless emails, TV commercials, mailouts, and the seemingly infinite amount of digital ads and placements, these concepts are still just being adapted to current technologies and trends. Master these things and say goodbye to the fear that you're only one disruption away from your sales tanking. The tactics will change, but the buyer's psychology remains.

What This All Means for You

Humor me for a moment and truly imagine what having all of this in place would do for you. What would this unlock in your business? How many packages would your team send out, and how many mail trucks per day would you fill, delivering your products to happy customers around the world?

What would having all of this in place allow you to do personally? What would it feel like, and what kind of peace of mind would it give you? Would it be exciting? If you had all of this, do you think you could scale your brand? Do you think you could 2x, 4x, or even 10x your sales? Would it be reasonable to think that you could turn your current yearly revenue into your new monthly revenue? I do.

I've seen it happen faster than you might think—not in five to ten years, sometimes not even in three to five years, but in one to three years, and occasionally even sooner. We've become absolutely obsessed with helping brands grow, and we live and breathe this stuff every single day. We've done it in almost every ecommerce niche imaginable, with hundreds of products and brands. Subscription boxes, boutiques, fashion brands, wigs, cold plunges, juice cleanses, books, toys, fitness programs, hunting gear, outdoors brands, kayaks, paddle boards, car parts, HVAC supplies, supplements—you name it, we've scaled it.

Will this book make your problems vanish into thin air and turn your life into nothing but rainbows and roses overnight? No, of course not. What I can assure you of is that doubling or even tripling your sales volume profitably is very achievable, and doing so can solve a multitude of problems.

If what I've laid out above makes your internal BS alarm screech louder than a thousand seven-year-olds on a sugar high at a birthday party, I completely understand. I've been there, too, and despite my skepticism, I have experienced amazing results for our business. I would be thinking the same thing if it weren't for the sheer number of brands successfully doing this, independent of anything we're involved with, and the significant impact this system has had on many brands we've worked with, creating tidal waves of revenue and transforming their lives.

What we've unpacked together in this book, though valuable, actionable, and comprehensive, is still only the tip of the iceberg, just a fraction of what we impart to store owners in our private coaching programs and what our team does at an almost instinctual level when solving problems for the brands we have the privilege of doing direct collaborations with.

If you're at all interested in some hands-on help from our team, I'd like to personally invite you to reach out. However, there are a few things you should know first.

First, good relationships are at the forefront of everything that we do. That means we always start with getting to know our clients. Below is a free gift and a link for you to book a call with our team completely free of charge. On this call, we will ask you several questions about your store and create space for you to ask any questions you may have for us. Think of it as a free coaching session. If there is a decent chance that we can help you hit your goals, at your request, our team will take a deep dive into your business and conduct an audit of your store to see how this system can be applied to your specific needs. Whether you're trying to hit your first $100k month or your first $100k day, wherever you're at, we'll build a plan that's customized to meet your goals.

After the audit is done and the plan is built, we will present that information to you. You then have a choice: you can implement the plan on your own, join one of our private coaching programs to get hands-on help implementing the plan, or you can partner with us and get a full team of ninja expert marketers on your account to help you scale. Either way, we are all good!

You'll get a complete breakdown of the system we use to get crazy results tailored to your brand. Why are we doing all of this? Yes, it's one way to get new clients—most people love the audit process so much and seeing how our systems can uniquely fit inside of what their brand already has going that they prefer that we do it for them.

But here's the catch, which you've likely been looking for this whole time: we can't help everyone. To ensure that the clients we do bring on are well taken care of, we limit the number of brands that we work with at any given time and hand-select the ones that we feel will have the best relationship with us.

At this point in time, our services aren't designed for brand-new beginners who have no clue what to sell or for people looking to get rich quickly. They aren't for people who are broke and have no money to invest in their business. They're for dedicated brand founders who are ready to go to the next level.

To claim your free gifts or contact our team, go to:
www.8figureowner.com/bonus
OR SCAN THE QR CODE:

Congratulations! You now have a crystal-clear understanding of what it looks like to become an eight-figure brand and know several practical techniques you can immediately use to shift your trajectory in that direction. Like any valuable information, it is only powerful to the extent that you use it. There are no shortcuts; success demands good old-fashioned hard work.

It has been an honor to spend this time with you, and I sincerely hope that your business journey only gets better from here. I believe good businesses can change the world and that your story matters greatly. Now, get out there and chart your path to becoming an *8 Figure Owner*.

THANK YOU FOR READING MY BOOK!

DOWNLOAD YOUR FREE GIFTS

Just to say thanks for buying and reading my book, I would like to give you a few free bonus gifts, no strings attached!

Scan the QR Code:

I appreciate your interest in my book, and value your feedback as it helps me improve future versions of this book. I would appreciate it if you could leave your invaluable review on Amazon.com with your feedback. Thank you!

www.ingramcontent.com/pod-product-compliance
Lightning Source LLC
LaVergne TN
LVHW020932090426
835512LV00020B/3324